Thank You for Calling Me Stupid

But God Planted a Seed in Me

Chaseray Harvey

Table of Contents

Acknowledgments

I WOULD LIKE to thank my Lord and Savior Jesus Christ for giving me purpose...this internal drive... this walk of development. Thank You for allowing me to reach this point in my life and shining Your Grace upon me. Thank You for giving me the attitude to believe in the vision of this book.

To my loving wife, Mattie Ricard Harvey thank you for totally transforming my life and helping me evolve into the man I am today. God brought you into my life to help me fulfill my purpose which is currently in progress. THANK YOU!

To my two loving daughters, Cassandra and Madison as well as my bonus son Tim...THANK YOU!

To my hard-working parents, Evelyn Johnson and Julius Harvey Jr, thank you for being my first amazing role models. You demonstrated hard-work, integrity, love, determination, and passion. Your legacy continues to be strong and will live on for GENERATIONS!

To my brothers, Curtis, Keith, Kennith and Julius, III for teaching me tenacity as well as showing me examples of right and wrong.

To my baby sister Sherry Harvey, an extraordinary woman and mother, thank you for keeping us together throughout the years.

To my Mentor, Dr. Leon Eichelberger and his amazing family, thank you for being a role model that every little eighth-grade boy deserves.

To my extended family, the Ricards as well as my work family, Thank you! To my oldest and dearest friends, and my new friends and business associates, I appreciate your confidence in my gifts along with the accolades of appreciation. I am blessed by our relationship which has helped me and my family pursue the philanthropic work we've been called to do. I am humbled at how God still gives me wisdom and continues to use me as a vessel to bring the best out of all of those I come in contact with. If it weren't for your support, my purpose would not be possible...THANK YOU ALL!

Dedication

To my Father, Mother, Brothers, and Sister for helping me create a "Teflon" mindset by calling me too stupid, which allowed me the opportunity to manifest God's seed of purpose that was planted inside me. I love you for helping me prepare myself for the world I would face.

Foreword

IN ADDITION TO my role as Pastor, I am honored to have taught middle school in the Harrisburg School District, Harrisburg, PA for 26 years. I met Jerome over 40 years ago at the Harrisburg Middle School where I was his eighth grade Social Studies Teacher. It was a tradition, on the first day of class, to introduce myself to the class as their father away from home and to let them know that I would treat them as my children expecting great things from them. To my surprise, Jerome took this proclamation literally, and that was the beginning of our Father/Son relationship. I took him under my wings and started mentoring him, instilling in him the value of love, respect, compassion, trust, education and the teachings and values of Jesus Christ.

As our relationship grew, I took him home to meet my wife and she fell in love with him. That day, he became our son. We didn't have children at the time, therefore, he was so excited and happy.

I saw something in Jerome that he didn't see in himself. He had potential and just needed direction. It became my quest to be that person to point him in the right direction.

A year later, we had our first child and that kind of bothered Jerome. When Xavier was born, Jerome wanted to know if he would still be our son. We assured him that he would always be our oldest son. Jerome and Xavier bonded well, and he became the big brother to Xavier and to our second son, Anwar.

As the years progressed, he grew in stature, wisdom, knowledge, and Christ. Not only did I mentor him in the educational arena but I also instilled in him the need for Christ to be in his life. He needed to walk upright before Christ and also walk upright before his peers.

As Jerome continued to move through high school, I was always a part of his life. We took him to family gatherings and family reunions. Our vacations were his vacations. He became a real Eichelberger.

After graduating from high school, he enrolled at Harrisburg Area Community College (HACC). After a year at HACC, he decided that he needed to leave Harrisburg. He had family in Houston, Texas and could get a new start there. Jerome was looking for something that could not be found in Harrisburg. He needed a different environment and Houston would be it. In his move to Houston, God continued to keep him covered with the blood of Jesus. In Houston, he finally found his calling in the men's fashion industry. God has richly blessed him and gave him success. In all of his accomplishments, I thank God that he is still humble, thankful, caring, and loving. His love for family and humanity is visible and live.

Jerome always reminds me that if I had not been in his life and planted, instilled, encouraged, loved on him, (and yes, put the belt to his behind), he wouldn't be where he is today. I thank God for our Father / Son relationship. I pray that he will continue to be humble, loving, and always put God at the head of his life, and continue to show love to others.

To my fellow readers, as you page through this memoir, I hope you can pick up some nuggets of wisdom, love, compassion, patience, and humility.

To Jerome, you've grown into all of that with the help of God. Remember that what people call you doesn't matter. The Word of God says, "You are fearfully and wonderfully made." They may have called you "**stupid**", but God called you **sophisticated, stylish and simply the best!**
Rev. Dr. Leon Eichelberger
Retired Pastor, Beulah Baptist Church

THANK YOU FOR CALLING ME STUPID...

Introduction

DID YOU HAVE a chance to check out the photo on the book cover? Which one of those handsome young guys do you think I am? See the shy kid in the picture with his eyes looking down to the ground? Yep. That's me. Jerome Chaseray Harvey. The other four guys are my four brothers. Starting from the top, left to right is Kennith, Curtis, Keith, and Julius. Notice how I am the only one looking down? I do not recall what was going through my mind at the time, but I know what I feel when I see the picture now. I was called "stupid" so many times while growing up and there were times I actually believed it. Reading, writing, and organizational skills have always been my weaknesses, but I have learned to embrace them and I have overcome as of today. I emphatically declare, **I AM NOT STUPID!**

When people say to me, "Hey, how's it going, Chaseray?" In the loudest, most boisterous voice I can muster, I ALWAYS respond with, "FANTASTIC, PHENOMENAL, UNBELIEVABLE, EXTRAORDINARY...ON A WHOLE 'NOTHA LEVELLLLLLL!!!" Some people laugh hysterically, and others just stare in pure amazement at how much I love life! Nothing can stop me; nothing can harm me and greatness surrounds me. To everyone who has ever called me "stupid"...Thank You! To everyone who has ever counted me out or mishandled me, Thank You! To all of the teachers who said I had a learning disability, Thank You! To everyone who made fun of me and never thought I would be anything in life, Thank You! Because of you I am stronger, wiser, better and winning every day.

There were so many remarkable things occurring on March 15, 1961, when I was born. I had no idea what was going to take place and how my life was going to evolve. Once you finish reading this book, you will see the evolution that has occurred in my life. I am extremely grateful for all of my experiences because they were preparing me to become who I am today. Some people may find it hard to believe that I was a shy kid growing up. Others will be shocked at what they will learn about me. Who knew little Jerome would grow to become Chaseray Harvey, successful businessman, loving husband, and father? God planted a seed in me, and I am blessed to be able to share what I've learned with the world.

Even through adversity, I've been blessed to relate to so many incredible people. God uses me every single day to help people collide with their purpose and go after their dreams. I look forward to helping you do that too as you peek inside my life's journey.

The purpose of this book is to:

1. **Reveal** some of the tough life lessons I've learned regarding love, sex, relationships and how helping others is one of the core secrets to monumental success.
2. **Expose** some of my "dirty little secrets" that may seem shocking at first, but in the end, you will be able to distinguish the endless possibilities you have at your disposal to activate

in order to live your best life right NOW regardless of past mistakes.

3. **Share** amazing testimonials of how God used me as a vessel to transform and impact the lives of so many people I've been honored to work with. Not to boast of how great I am, but to remind you of how one life can impact a generation.

4. **Encourage** you that NOTHING is an issue or a problem. In other words, no matter what you have been through or how dark your past may have been, there is NOTHING that you can't accomplish if your heart is in it. Your mind has to be focused and your spirit has to embrace a higher power. My higher power just happens to be Jesus Christ.

My job is not to convert you, but to strengthen you in the areas where you may be weak or feel like you don't deserve love, happiness or success. My goal is to bring your strengths to the forefront. You deserve all that life has to offer you, and you certainly can have it all.

At the end of this book, you will be set free from limitations such as doubt, fear and lack of hope. So grab your favorite cup of coff ee or beverage choice, along with something to write with and an open mind. You may laugh out loud or shed a tear as I share some of the most amazing times of my life with you. Allow my life's reflections to help you avoid pitfalls and pain so you can live the best life you can live.

The hustle game is how you made ends meet in the '70s. We started having rent parties and sold beer, cigarettes, and alcohol. It was wrong, but don't judge me until you hear the whole story.

1

Meet the Harveys

I REMEMBER BEING in kindergarten, sleeping on the blue mat and having recess. I didn't care for school that much. It was hard and the only thing I enjoyed doing was art and gym class. Once I received my report card for the first time, I was so excited to open it up. "WOW, YES!" I didn't understand report cards earlier in my life until the third grade. I couldn't wait to make it home! Every minute that passed until school let out, I was so excited to share my results with my family! As soon as the bell rang, I ran extremely fast to our house as it was right across the street from my school, Woodward Elementary. Once I arrived home, I was jumping up-and-down and said, "Oh, Mom and Dad! Will you look at what I have!?" My brothers were already there showing their report cards to our mother. She was happy with my brothers' results as she gave them positive acknowledgments. I said, "Mom, you must see my report card!" She said, "Hold on, Baby Boy. I'll be with you in one second. I'm looking at your brother's report card right now." I said with so much confidence, "It's okay because you are going to be very happy with me because I believe my report card is better than my brothers!" It was finally my turn to talk to my mother. "Baby Boy, show me exactly what you received." I handed her the report card and I excitedly said to her, "I am Dynamic and Fantastic!" She said, "Why would you say that?" "Take a look at my report card! It's better than my brothers and I'm dynamic and fantastic!" She opened up the report card and said, "No, boy you stupid!" "Why would you say that to me, Mom?" "Because you have D's and F's on your report card but your brothers received A's and B's. At that point, my brothers bust out laughing. They laughed and laughed all day. From that day forward I would be branded as, "stupid". From that day forward, there was never a time that I wasn't being ridiculed by my siblings.

It all began in 1961 when I was born in the Harrisburg Hospital into a family that during that time it was my Dad, Julius, my Mom, Evelyn, my brothers Curtis, Keith, Kennith and Julius Harvey. My Sister, Sherry came along a few years later. We were a very proud family that believed in love and hard work. We believed that one day the hard work would pay off for us. As little boys, our parents would teach us not only to work hard but to cook, clean, braid hair, sew on a Singer sewing machine and make ice cream from

From left to right, Curtis, Keith, Kennith, Julius, Sherry and ME!

My Mom and Dad

scratch. Many of those activities I still engage in, therefore, I am forever grateful for those valuable life lessons my parents taught me. When our parents would go out to party, we'd bake a cake. My parents were furious when they came home and found out that we were baking while they were gone. That was a "no-no"! We were disciplined every time we did it since it was extremely dangerous. My parents would have house parties and become intoxicated while entertaining the guests who came over to party. My brothers and I were often referred to as, "The Jackson 5". So that's where my life began. For the most part, being a Harvey was a respected thing and something to be proud of. Why? Because we could do just about anything. I remember quite well when The Harvey's were the family of all families in Harrisburg, Pennsylvania. We were a tough family. We fought each other for toys using hammers and screwdrivers! At times, it was all out war in my home. We would go into the basement, turn off the lights and then throw iron or other metal objects at one another so badly that it was normal for someone to end up hurt. Our "basement wars" was a weekly game we would play.

My childhood home is on the left

We lived in a very modest and small home at 909 North 18th Street in Harrisburg, Pennsylvania.It was a three-bedroom home, and my parents stayed in the front room. Julius and I stayed in the middle room. Curtis, Keith, and Kennith stayed in the back room where we made the balcony into a bedroom, and they slept on the bunk bed.

As a child, I was curious about so many things and a lot of times very hungry for candy or pretty much anything for that matter. I used to love gazing out my bedroom window during the summer while my mother was at work. Some days I would really crave candy, but my babysitter refused to give it to me. Since I couldn't find any, I started eating the paint chippings from the window seal. I would sit on the window seal for hours until one day someone caught me. During that time, paint had lead in it, and if I didn't stop, eventually I would have been sick due to lead poisoning. I didn't eat enough for it to harm me, but I ate enough to where even to this day I experience tremors in my hands from time to time. I also used to put money in my mouth. One day I ended up swallowing a dime and my family rushed me to the doctor. He said I would be fine, but there was nothing they could do. I would just have to wait until it passed through my system. God continued to look out for me even when I didn't realize what I was doing.

At a very young age, I got into a lot of bad things like smoking, drinking, stealing and breaking into cars. At the time, I didn't know any better. I never stole anything big and NEVER from my parents, siblings, aunts, uncles or cousins. I remember thinking that I was grown in my little mind. My older brother, Curtis introduced me to older women and the hustle game. My Dad once abandoned us leaving my mother to pay for food and housing. The hustle game is how you made ends meet in the '70s. My brothers and I started having rent parties and sold beer, cigarettes, and alcohol. It was wrong, but don't judge me until you hear the whole story.

I started drinking and smoking unbeknownst to my parents. I thought this was the way to live watching how we lived paycheck to paycheck and witnessing my parents working so hard to take care of us. I would do everything I could to escape to my cousins, Marvin and Greg's house, where I would drink and smoke weed. There were so many times we would sit there daydreaming about our future and one day being a successful person. We would dream and pray about our future all the time. We called ourselves, "The 3 Musketeers".

As time went on my mother worked for Blue Cross Blue Shield, and my father worked for Goodyear. We had babysitters that watched us every day after school, and we would drive them nuts! We were so out of control until we would tie them up and then go outside and play. We were so out of control that no one wanted to keep us, so we looked after each other. I don't remember how old my oldest brother, Curtis or my twin brothers, Keith, and Kennith were at the time, but one thing I do know is that they always loved women, sports and making trouble—in that order! Curtis was a ladies' man. He was a very handsome young man who played drums in the band and was a high school football star. He inspired me to play sports and become great at it. My brother, Keith was very focused and determined growing up. He was always protective of the family. He also loved fashion and luxury cars that he kept super clean. To me, Keith was the REAL "Super Fly", and he dressed like it. My brother, Kennith was the strong one in the family. He was the go-getter, the handyman, a leader and very supportive. Although all of my brothers served in the United States Army, Kennith was the one who took it seriously from day one. He was, "Mr. G.I. Joe" and there was NOTHING he wouldn't do. I learned about fashion and cars from Keith, but I learned fearlessness and drive from Kennith. I remember a time my brother Kennith was braiding my brother Julius's hair in the front living room and he was always making fun of me and calling me stupid. Later, when he was sitting down having his hair braided, I took a pair of pliers and cracked him over the head and I said, "NOW who's stupid!" My mom beat me like I had stole something! My brother Julius was my first best friend. He taught me so many things like how to dress, how to focus and succeed by achieving one goal at a time. He used to have a picture of a green Grand Prix above his bed, and eventually, he owned one just like it. He used the power of focus to get exactly what he wanted. I am so proud of all of my brothers. In their own special way, they gave me the best examples of my childhood that would pay me extreme dividends later in life. At times, Julius and Curtis stole from me and my family, but I always found a way to forgive them. Even when my brother Keith beat me with a foldable chair I found a way to still love him. I love all my brothers even when they believed I was the stupid one. I told them, "One day, I will become someone you all will be proud of."

My Sister, Sherry

My Baby Sister, Sherry was the most beautiful baby I had ever seen. I was six years old when she came home from the Hospital, and everything changed immediately. Sherry Elaine Harvey, the princess of the house full of rambunctious little boys. She changed everything about our family dynamic because now there was a girl in the house. Although my mother was the Queen of the home, everything changed now that we had a girl in the house. My brothers and I were extremely overprotective when it came to our baby sister. She had her army of five big brothers to protect her. When she came into our lives, everything changed for the better. Even still to this day, she is the glue that holds the family together. Thank you, Sis!

My First "A"

For the very first time while I was in Fifth Grade, I received an "A" on a spelling test. I was so excited when I arrived home and showed my mother, father, and brothers my spelling test. They were so happy for me. That was a proud moment for me, so I decided to share it with my cousins, Greg and Marvin. I went over to their house and they were standing on the front porch. I showed them my spelling test...my very first A! They were both honor roll students. They looked at the test and started laughing hilariously as they fell to the ground. I asked them, "Why are you laughing so hard?" They both said, "Your spelling test is correct, but you misspelled your name!" This was so demoralizing and hurtful. I tried so hard to achieve my first A and once I thought I achieved it, I really didn't. That was a hurting feeling but that moment was also a game-changer later down the road of life. Even though they laughed at me, they really helped me. At the time I didn't know it. Why? When adversity came my way I embraced it. The tough times they put me through only built up my resistance. It allowed me to take on adversity in a very positive and motivating way.

The Lone "Black" Ranger

I remember the day when my mother chose to move me out of public school into St. Margaret Mary, a very distinguished private, Catholic School in Harrisburg. The day my mother checked my sister and I into St. Margaret Mary, we met with the head Nun of the school, Sister Mary. I remember her calling Sister Ann to take me to the 6th grade classroom. This school was so different from the school I came from. We walked down the hall to the classroom door then walked right out crying hysterically! I ran to my mother while Sister Ann stood there and they asked me, "What's wrong?" I replied, "There are all white people in the classroom!" I cried, but my mother would not budge on her decision. I was the ONLY black person in the class.

Later that same year another black girl joined the class. Even my baby sister, Sherry, was the only black person in her class, and at first, it was devastating. I couldn't see it at the moment, however, becoming a student at St. Margaret Mary provided some of the most amazing times in my life. The culture of the school taught me how to be a better person just by following the dress code. Our football and basketball teams were successfully undefeated. I learned about Jesus Christ, His work on the cross, the Ten Commandments and even the sacrament of Holy Communion. It was one of the most amazing experiences a young boy could have ever had. Now I know exactly why my mother took me out of public school. At that time, I was so frustrated and so lost. I just knew in my heart I was going to find a way not to be that "stupid" guy anymore. I was determined to prove everybody wrong about my academic background. My mom wanted to save me and help enhance my future. I struggled when I was in public school, but when I went to Catholic School, I received the attention I needed to become a better student. My Mom was a genius for moving me to such an incredible environment because the pay off has been extraordinary! Thank you, Mom, for saving my life and the sacrifice of your time to make a better life for me and my sister, Sherry.

All About My Neighborhood

From the age of nine, Life presented a lot of different perceptions to me. I was raised in a family with a military structure since my father fought in the Korean War. I was the youngest of four boys, and my sister hadn't been born yet, so my father's philosophy about how life was to be lived was very concise. From haircuts to when we ate meals to ironing our clothes and making up beds… we lived that military life. "Yes, Sir," "No, Sir," "Yes, Ma'am," "No, Ma'am" was normal vocabulary in my home. My father was a very strong man and groomed in the art of discipline and the code of respect. Discipline was a major core value that my Father instilled in my siblings and I. There were times when we would sit down to eat dinner. My Father knew that food was scarce so he would fill our plates full of food and we had to sit there until every last bit of it was gone. He would always say, "You don't know where your next meal might come from..." and that was so true. One of the first things I discovered about our family dynamic was the fact that he had high respect for my mother. He always told us, "No matter what you see me do, ALWAYS respect your mother." His words stuck with me even to this day. His discipline was firm with all of us when we would act out and behave badly. Sometimes he would use hangers, water hoses or anything closest to him to discipline us. Sometimes he would send one of us to grab the large switch from the nearest tree and say, "Bring it back to me." We all knew what that meant, but I found out what discipline and accountability was all about. Now, I know some of you may think it was abuse but actually, that was his way of showing his love to keep is out of trouble when we became adults. He never intended to hurt us, but he did want us to behave. Even though we would all be disciplined for staying up late and cooking cakes without my parents knowing, it often felt like I was the one receiving the most discipline. The Harvey Boys were always up to something.

Where we lived was approximately six blocks from the ghetto, but I had more of a middle-class upbringing. Being on the edge of the projects two houses over was our elementary school, Woodward Elementary. There was also a corner store called "Sam's" I discovered gambling for the very first time. I watched men take each other's money...it was one of the most extraordinary things I ever saw at that time. There was also a pool hall, and I was intrigued as a young boy watching these men play with such intensity and talking so much smack to each other. All of the neighborhood kids and teens would come to the pool hall. I guess you could consider Sam's the Community Center for the edge of the projects. Sam was a very nice man with a very nice daughter. They lived right above the pool hall and store. Sam's place was THE SPOT, especially during the summer. That's where I watched guys gamble while playing Blackjack, Dominos, Roll Dice and Pitch Quarters. It was an exciting time! The other kids and I would play Table Hockey, DodgeBall, Wall Ball for hours and even spent time at Woodward Elementary school playground where there was a basketball court where we'd play pick-up games. I remember the summer when Joe Frazier and Muhammad Ali were set to fight in the world-famous match, "Thrilla in Manilla." There were two teenagers at that time who could pass for grown men were set to fight each other. We created our OWN championship between these two guys. They were all set with boxing gloves ready for war. The entire neighborhood came to view the spectacle and wanted these two boy-men to replicate the major fight that was set to happen between Frazier and Ali. This was so exciting for me...for all of us. You could taste the anticipation as we watched and waited for the fight to begin. Finally, the makeshift bell rings and these two go giants go at it. Their gloves violently smacked across each other's faces...it was surreal. Shortly after that, some of the kids in the area near uptown on the Southside of the hill established gangs. I was able to identify the gangs and later found my brothers were gang members, too. They would go around picking fights and completely knock people out for no reason. The Harveys established a strong reputation for being strong and not backing down from a fight. There was one guy by the name of R.W. who was tight with my brother, Kennith. He was considered one of the best "Knockout Specialists" in the city. I didn't grow up in the hood, but I grew up down the street from it.

Strong Mind, Winning Mind

I remember when I was finally old enough to secure a summer job, my brothers and I would cut grass for $2.00 an hour. I was so excited the first year that I was able to do it because every year my brothers would do it and I couldn't because I was too young. Finally, I was old enough to work and help earn extra money for the family. I didn't enjoy cutting down the tall grass, but I did whatever I had to do to help support my family. We did this every single year, and I enjoyed the fact that I received payment. We had to give a portion of our earnings to our parents, but they allowed us to keep the rest which I appreciated. We struggled throughout our childhood because my father was in and out of a job, while my mother was busy raising us and going to work as well. During these times, it was very difficult for a man of valor to secure a good job in the '60s. My brothers and I became providers for the house after my father decided to leave my mother for a younger woman. Our house was always on the verge of being foreclosed on, so my brothers and I started having house parties just to stay afloat. Remember, we were a very well-known family, so we started having house parties in the basement setup just like a nightclub. There was a dollar cover charge plus we'd charge another dollar for alcohol and beer and made a killing selling cigarettes. Every Friday and Saturday we'd bring about $300-$500 to help pay the mortgage. Those parties were great, and we'd pack the folks in there like sardines. We played music by *Earth, Wind and Fire*, *Bootsy Collins, Rick James, Ohio Players, Brass Construction, James Brown, The Sugarhill Gang, Curtis Blow* and of course *The Jackson Five*...the music was always on point. We were famous for mixing Moonshine with Hawaiian Punch and we'd charge a dollar per cup. We were good at convincing the neighborhood teenagers to talk to other teenagers about coming to the party. Everyone always looked forward to our parties because they knew we threw the best one on the block. Throwing house parties was the thing that kept our house afloat. I'm totally amazed at our business ability back then. I don't think any of us had a clue how selling cigarettes, alcohol and throwing successful, profitable house parties put our entrepreneurial spirit on display. I had no clue that I was being groomed to be successful in business. I don't have to sell alcohol or throw house parties anymore, but I am grateful for the tough times which taught me how to succeed in life against all odds.

One summer we started working at a retirement home uptown on Front Street. I was really excited because I worked with other teenagers supporting the nursing staff by cleaning the rooms and removing trash. Every day on our lunch break we'd get high and then come back to finish up for the day. One day one of the guys said he had a real good deal that could get us real high. We all agreed to try it. He pulls out this piece of paper with yellow dots on it. He told us to put the paper on our tongues and wait a few minutes. He assured us that it wasn't going to do nothing bad to nobody, but we underestimated the effects of what this "break" would do. So after about an hour, it took effect, and it nearly blew my mind. I just started mentally and physically tripping. I started talking like a duck to anybody who spoke to me. Before I knew it, I was paranoid and afraid right there on the job. I asked the guy what he did to me, and he said he gave me something called, "Paper Acid" or in medical terms, LSD. As the hours went by I felt worse and worse. I knew I had to find my way home. I called my father and begged him to pick me up. He asked me why I wanted to come home and I told him the room was spinning…it seemed as if the entire world was spinning. I pleaded with him to pick me up because I felt absolutely terrible! Once my dad finally arrived, he said, "What do you want me to do? Do I need to take you to the doctors?" I said, "No, No, No…please just take me home. I think I just need to lay down." We arrived home, and I remember him taking me upstairs to his room. He told me to lay in the bed until I felt better because he was headed back to work. I laid there, and the entire room just kept spinning all day long. I vowed to myself I would never take acid paper again!

Another challenging time in my childhood was when my cousin, Yvonne, introduced me to liquid hash. You'd spread this "honey-like" substance on marijuana paper, add some marijuana, roll it and smoke it. I even found myself trying cocaine and speed one or two times, but I never did crack. I was told that once I did crack, I would be addicted virtually overnight. I was headed down the destructive path of being addicted to drugs. I almost knew what it was like to be addicted to drugs. Whenever I would use, I became vulgar and obscene, and people would simply say, "It's his decision." As time went on, I realized that using drugs makes your mind weak and you'd do anything you could to get high. Drugs make you feel successful without doing the work. I didn't realize it at the time, but my mental capacity was stronger than any drug overtaking me as it has taken over the lives of so many people I used to take drugs with. Even though I was reckless and irresponsible at times, God protected the seed that He planted in me. I thank God for protecting me from the danger that I could see and danger I had no clue about. I probably should be a drug addict to this day but thank God for a strong mind and the will to win.

My First Funeral

My parents and I traveled to New York City with my Uncle Robert, Aunt Ada, Aunt Eloise, and Aunt Zula. This was my first clear understanding of what a funeral was all about. My Great Aunt Evelyn, who my mother was named after, passed away. We traveled to Aunt Moselle's house, my Mom's other sister, where we stayed before the funeral. The evening before the funeral, we all were entertaining each other and drank all night. I drowned myself in alcohol to avoid the fear of seeing a dead person the next day. The day of the funeral, we arrived to the church and sat on the front pew right in front of the coffin. No one knew I was intoxicated and didn't sleep much the night before. I laid my head on my mother's shoulder and started moaning. Everyone thought that I was moaning and suffering because of the passing of my Aunt. I started moaning even louder and making the scene more serious concerning the passing of my aunt. The truth is I had a severe hangover and was completely EXHAUSTED! I made so much noise until eventually I was removed from the funeral because everyone thought I was mourning the loss of my aunt. (I did not really know her at all.) After I sobered up, I told my family the truth that I was intoxicated and sleepy with a massive hangover. Everyone paused and stared at me and then at each other and burst into extreme laughter! Even though it was a very difficult time for our family, that moment of laughter was right on time.

I knew I was going to make a positive impact on people one day. I was open to learning and excited about living an extraordinary life.

2

The Learning Opportunity:
Life Lessons

I TRULY ENJOYED the life lessons my mother taught all of us as well as my father. One of the most valuable lessons I learned was attending church and being able to dress up in a nice suit, tie, dress shirt, and dress shoes. We were members of Worship God Methodist Church and even though I didn't always understand what was going on as I sat in the pew listening to the pastor, I now realize I took my church experience for granted. Later in life, I realized that even though I didn't understand my pastor's interpretation at the time, what he said was very important. Having God in your life is a key ingredient in achieving monumental success in life. I was completely disconnected and had a difficult time embracing church because I perceived the pastor along with the rest of the church people to be old, outdated and in many cases just plain spooky! I took for granted the weekly learning opportunities that I had the privilege of receiving. The seed that God planted in me was being watered even if I did not reap the harvest right away. After I became a man, I was determined that church was a way of keeping me honest and my family healthy and together. The sense of community that the church provides is so powerful because if it is done the right way, it keeps families together under one common goal of learning integrity and respect.

One thing I always loved was Easter Sunday. It was a time where people would buy suits, and little girls had poofy dresses along with lace socks and patent leather shoes. Folks would be dressed to the nines! It was always a big celebration of people honoring the resurrection of Jesus Christ. I think the Easter Sunday experience has been tarnished over the years but every spring I look forward to it. Some parents worked hard and over-extended themselves to buy these extraordinary outfits for their kids. For big families like mine, it was very challenging for parents who bought all these fancy clothes, but my mother and father would somehow pull it off every year. They would even go so far as to invest in painting dozens of eggs for our yearly Easter Egg Hunt and a phenomenal meal would be cooked to perfection! Even Thanksgiving, Christmas and especially birthdays were truly extraordinary times.

I was taught the art of discipline from day one. Some folks don't learn about discipline until they acquire their first job, but I remember my mother and father teaching us discipline in many ways. For example, when my parents purchased new furniture, they would put plastic over it to shield against dirt. My siblings and I knew the furniture was off limits and that plastic was a "do not touch" sign that we never violated. They even had plastic runners on the floor from the front door to the kitchen. Anytime we walked into the house we had to take our shoes off. My mom also had a beautiful China cabinet with "the untouchables." These were items that were treated like they were a part of a culinary museum and my siblings and I knew full well that "the untouchables" were off-limits. The learning opportunities that my parents passed on to me are invaluable and too numerous to mention. They instilled genuine respect and a bazaar hunger for hard work. They did this because they wanted us to cherish the things we acquired because we worked hard for it. My mother didn't have the plastic on the furniture just to keep it clean, but she did it so we would learn to cherish the things we worked hard for. She wanted to enjoy the furniture she worked so hard for as long as she could, and she knew if she had not covered it, it might have been destroyed before the end of the week. As I look back, I realize how much I lacked appreciation for the things she purchased for our family and the learning opportunities presented to us. Nowadays, I see how children are growing up entitled, and there is a huge gap in parents being appreciated for what they do for their kids.

Another lesson I learned was from my father to BE ON TIME! My father was extremely punctual when he worked for PPG and Goodyear Tire Company. He would go to work at least two hours before his actual shift started. He would sit in the lobby and wait for his shift to begin. His supervisors were always intrigued by the fact that he would do this for 30 plus years. He spent an incredible amount of time focusing on the task at hand so that he could be one of the best if not the best at his profession. I have not seen this kind of work ethic in any profession. Punctuality is so key for me because my father set the standard. I had to make a few adjustments over the years because depending on the relationship I was in at the time, I have not been the most punctual person. Initially, I did not implement this regiment and structure into my life as an adult. I am truly grateful to my dad for showing me that a real man always shows up on time. As children, my siblings and I were very lazy, and if we weren't playing we wanted to relax! We played extremely hard and worked hard, too, but instead of sleeping, we would stay up all night watching TV and talking. By morning, my mother had the most challenging time waking us up for school the next day. My parents were always saying, "Go to bed on time, so you can get up on time." We didn't listen because we wouldn't even stay in our beds. We didn't have cell phones at the time so we would go and raise up the window and talk to the neighbors next door for hours. If we weren't talking to the neighbor, we were talking to each other…man those were good times!

My Dad was the first person with a CB radio in his car because he traveled so much from city to city. This way he could stay ahead of the police. Believe it or not, my Dad would wear sunglasses at night to see better. For real Dad? My brother Keith took it to the next level with a portable cell phone with a boomerang antenna on the trunk, sunroof top, diggin' the scene lead with a gangsta lean, WHOO WHOO!

My father had a military background so every morning he would yell, "It's time to get up!" And after saying it a few times, he would fill a bucket up full of water and throw it on us! We were SOAKED from head to toe, and we'd have to flip the mattress over so it would not be wet when we came home from school! We hoped he wouldn't throw more water on us, but he knew we wouldn't wake up so the next morning he would throw more water on us. Now BOTH sides of the mattress were completely soaked, and many nights we slept on a wet mattress all because we could not wake up on time. The "waterworks" went on for quite some time until we became conditioned to make sure that when he said, "WAKE UP!" We immediately woke up with our feet on the floor just like they do in the military. We were ready to go when it was time. I couldn't understand why my Father did this at the time, but now I know why he did it. He was teaching us the art of discipline and the responsibility of being on time. Now, I did not continue the water-throwing tradition with my children, but I trust that my father did the best job he knew how when it came to discipline. The moral of the story is this, don't allow water to be thrown on you because you refuse to show up on time to your destiny appointments.

My father cut our hair every Sunday morning. As I grew older, I started noticing all the different hairstyles. Since my father was the barber of the house, I always asked him for the latest hairstyle. He would say, "Have a seat." and would cut off all my hair off. I was totally bald! I would say, "Dad, you told me you was giving me that hairstyle!" "I did, now you can imagine any style you want now that you have a bald head because you and your brothers don't like keeping your hair combed! When you wake up every morning, look in the mirror and imagine ANY hairstyle you want!" **Thanks, Dad for setting the standard and showing us you can have anything if we put forth the effort to take care of it, if not someone else will set the standard for you.**

One of the most wonderful pastimes of my childhood was putting together puzzles on the dining room table which was our family entertainment, and we loved every minute of it! My mother loved to help keep our minds stimulated with the puzzles. They were always beautiful scenic pictures, and we would try to solve them as quickly as possible. If we weren't solving puzzles, we had a deck of cards playing *Blackjack 21*, *Bingo*, and *Tic Tac Toe*. When times became a little better, we were able to buy *Monopoly*, *Checkers*, and *Chess*. We always played wonderful games like *Hide* and *Go Seek*, *Red Light*, *Green Light*, and *Hopscotch*. I had a blast with my family because it was a great way to pass the time.

I didn't really know what it was like to have the experience of shopping for new clothes because most of my clothes were hand-me-downs. My brother Curtis would always receive the newest clothes that would eventually be passed down to me after my other brothers wore it first. Curtis would pass down his sneakers which would have a hole in them. I would have to wear about three pairs of socks and put cardboard at the bottom of the shoe just to keep my feet warm during the winter. Back then, Chuck Taylors were very popular, and kids loved them. The only time any of us would receive our own pair of sneakers was if it was our birthday or when my parents had a significant amount of extra money to spend on us. I always looked forward to Christmas even though the gifts were very limited. I was happy to receive a nice handkerchief and a good meal. Perhaps I would receive one toy, but I was just glad to be a part of a loving family. We all loved each other, and that was the greatest gift of all. My parents worked so hard just to keep a roof over our heads. My father worked multiple jobs. Jobs in

Harrisburg were hard to come by, but once he was able to find steady employment, he came back home.

I recall one time when my father left my mother. We had no idea where he was so we asked the Red Cross to help us find him. At times he would travel to Houston for a while to help provide for the family. There was so much going on at the time that I didn't know about but he finally came back, and things seemed to be okay. About a month or two later, I was riding in the car with my mother down 17th Street on our way home, and I asked her, "Where is Daddy?" She replied, "He's at work at Goodyear." I said in a quiet voice, "OK" but I knew something just didn't feel right. As we continued down the street, suddenly I saw him! I said, "Mom, there's Dad!" and she said emphatically, "No, your dad's at work." I wasn't trying to be disrespectful, but I KNEW I saw my Dad. Again, I said, "Mom, that was Dad." And she replied a little more irritated at this point, "No, your Father is at work!" I exclaimed, "Mom, that was Dad!" and I was very adamant about the fact that it was my father. At this point my mom was upset, and she told me, "If I turn this car around and that's not him, I'm beatin' yo butt!" So she whipped the Deuce and a Quarter with the black top and Crème interior around, and sure enough, there was my Dad. I remember this defining moment so vividly. I witnessed my Father pushing a carriage with another lady. My mother slammed on the breaks and went nuts right there on the sidewalk. She cussed both of them out...calling them all kinds of names. She was adamant about wanting to know who the child was and they stood there shocked that they were caught. I can't remember much after that, but I do remember my dad coming back to the house. He and my mom had a vicious fight, but my father denied everything. Many years later we learned that the child he was pushing in that carriage was his son. My dad went on to have two other children out of wedlock. This was devastating for my family, but I knew there was a learning opportunity for me. I appreciate the fact that my dad did his best to take care of his responsibilities. He may not have gone about it the right way, but I trust that he had good intentions. I am not excusing his behavior but as a man who has made my own mistakes, I understand.

While they are having this feud, I was still in the car with my leg trapped by the seat belt...COME ON, MAN!

3

Come On, Man!

I CANNOT TELL you how many times God has miraculously spared my life over the years. I know without a shadow of a doubt that I should be dead because of some of the reckless decisions I've made and some of the situations I had no control over. I become emotional and humbled when I think of all the times when I could have lost my life, but God saved me in order to be a blessing to others.

The Drag Race

Growing up, I spent a lot of time with my cousin, Alan. We spent many nights bar hopping in his green Chrysler Charger. I spent a lot of time running across State Street Bridge and to the Harrisburg Park nonstop. I could run for miles nonstop, and I actually enjoyed it. I enjoyed people being amazed that I could go around, up and down those massive hills for an extended period of time and then finish strong at the fastest pace I could muster. On the days I wasn't running or barhopping, I would spend hours hanging out in the park socializing, smoking weed and drinking beer as I watched the girls go by. One day my brother, Curtis and I challenged my cousin to a drag race. My brother had an extraordinary Black and Gold Trans Am called "Smoky the Bandit" with mag wheels…what an amazing car!

Jolted Teen Held For Observation

A city teen-ager early Friday was being held for observation at Polyclinic Medical Center after a one-car accident at Seventh and Division streets, according to police and hospital reports.

Jerome Harvey, 17, of 909 N. 16th St., was a passenger in a car driven by his brother, Curtis, 21, of the same address, police said.

Harvey was traveling north on Seventh Street about 8:40 p.m., police reported, when he lost control of his car while attempting to make a left turn onto Division Street.

The car hit the curb in front of the Uptown Plaza Shopping Center, causing the vehicle to flip over, police said.

Ready…Set…GO! Right at the start of the race on the State Street Bridge, my brother took the lead and continued to accelerate his speed to nearly 100 miles per hour. We forcibly turned onto Seventh Street at an even higher rate of speed, and I'm SCREAMING out the window, "MAD PUPPY!" and he's screaming, "MAD DOG!"… it was EXHILARATING! Division Street had a left turn at the end of it. We were going so fast when suddenly, we approached the left turn and hit the curb sideways. The car flipped a number of times right into the parking lot. All I can remember is my face hit the dirt as the car flipped over. Once we finally stopped moving, my body was hanging out of the passenger window of the car trapped by my seatbelt. My brother, Keith was in the car behind us with Cousin Alan, and they came running to the parking lot to make sure we were good. My older brother Curtis climbed out of the car and seemed to be okay, but I wasn't. I was stuck in the seat belt inside the car. They told me to keep laying there until the ambulance arrived. All of a sudden, my brother Keith and Curtis started arguing because Keith was upset that Curtis had put my life in danger. While they are having this feud, I was still in the car with my leg trapped by the seat belt…COME ON, MAN! Suddenly, a "God moment" occurred…miraculously, my brother Curtis used animalistic strength to disconnect the seat belt from the car! That amazed me because we all know that seat belts are designed to stay put but somehow my big brother pulled the seatbelt from the car. He quickly dragged me away from the car just moments before the car caught on fire. I don't remember much of what happened at the scene of the accident, but moments later I noticed I was in the ER and they began to work on me. It was annoying and painful because I suffered many injuries including having a hole in my jaw along with several of my teeth missing. Because of the adrenaline pumping through my body because I had no idea that my body was in so much pain. The doctors started working on my face and sewing up my jaw. As time went on, my body was incredibly sore. I also suffered a spinal injury and was unable to sit up straight for several weeks. The doctor assured my family that I would be okay, but it would take weeks before I could sit or stand upright. He also stated in addition to the injuries that I was extremely intoxicated, and I could've lost my life. It was very clear that we were drunk having downed a six-pack of Colt 45, several glasses of Thunderbird and we smoked at least two joints right before the accident. If wasn't for me being intoxicated, I wouldn't have relaxed right before the crash. So here I am…stuck in bed or lounging on the couch for weeks until I was able to sit or stand up straight. Come On, MAN, I should be dead from that drag racing experience, and I vowed to God if He would heal me from my injuries I would NEVER do THAT again. He saved my life and healed my body. I even have a WINNING smile! I don't look like what I have been through. Only a great God can work miracles like that.

The Heater

I have so many short stories I could tell you about how God saved my life over the years but let me tell you about another time when my brother Julius and I could have died in a fire. One night, he and I were asleep in the basement of our house using a portable heater because it was so cold. The heater was sitting dangerously close to the end of the couch, and suddenly it caught on fire. Smoke quickly filled the entire basement, and then God intervened again. I know He woke my mother up because she made her way to the basement just in time to rescue us from the smoke-filled basement. That was such a remarkable moment that my family and I constantly reflect on to celebrate the goodness of God. We should have been killed but God worked another miracle, and for that, I am forever grateful. That's why I don't have time to be discouraged. Even when life happens to me or to those around me, I don't have a problem saying, "Come on, Man…God has been too amazing to us to ever doubt his power and grace on us!"

Next Level in Life

The first time I was exposed to sex was when I was playing basketball for the middle school. As a young boy, my friends and I were always talking about kissing girls and having sex with them. I was terrified at the thought of having sex but let me tell you about my first time. One day, some of my teammates and I were riding home from a basketball tournament in the station wagon car. The cheerleaders always went on the road with us. In fact, even during football season, the stars of the team like the quarterback or the running back were always kissing girls.

I enjoyed eavesdropping on the "locker room talk" of the football and basketball stars boasting about how many girls they had actually been with. I had so many questions because I was completely infatuated with the opposite sex. I tried my best to become more appealing to the cheerleaders, even the girls in the car. I felt defeated because I didn't feel I was attractive enough like some of the other guys. On top of that, I heard all the horror stories about getting girls pregnant or catching a disease, and that scared me for a long time. But then, I grew up. As I grew older, I established a "relationship" with several young ladies who taught me good lessons which helped me become the man that I am today. They helped me respect women to this day. I am grateful for Joe and his family who drove all the way from the suburbs to pick me up and drop me off every day for practices and games. I'm so thankful for helping an inner-city kid enjoy playing sports for an extraordinary school with an undefeated football and basketball team! It was not just a moment of being exposed to big accomplishments, but it was the fact that my entire life was transformed. I was blessed to be able to see a better part of life from a religious perspective as well as a family giving of their time. Thank you, Carman and Father Joe!

There was another young lady that I had a short relationship with who was older than me. She was a senior and I was in the 10th grade and I went to her prom. I think she really wanted me to date her because she had so many other guys who tried to be with her. She was known as "Jackie from Uptown". She was considered "off limits" based on where she lived. There were always rival gangs in that area so I literally had to sneak uptown just to see her. We had a brief but fun relationship where we talked a lot. Because she was older than me, I was intrigued by her level of intelligence. She ended up graduating and attending college at the University of Pittsburgh. One time, I drove to Pittsburgh to spend the night with her. Even though that relationship didn't last long, I really valued what we had and I learned a lot about women after being with her. Then I moved onto another young lady who caused my "stock" with women to go up. My brother Julius was talking to a young lady and she had a friend who lived in Steelton. Even after Julius stopped talking to his lady friend and I would still travel back to Steelton to spend time with her in my mother's car. Her car was like my mobile apartment because it was a huge vehicle with a lot of interior space where I would always entertain. Here's where God protected me: we would be drinking all night in the backseat of the car until the wee hours of the morning. In my ignorance, I would drive back home after being out all night. That was so dangerous because at any time someone could've pulled up and caught us in the backseat of a car! One night, I overslept and had to be back at a certain time. I was extremely tired and I wrecked my mother's car. I messed up one side of my mother's car and I knew I was in a world of trouble. So the next morning, I parked the car on the corner and my mom went out to go to work.

When she saw it was damaged she came to my room and woke me up saying, "What have you done to my car?" I told her, "I don't know. Someone must have sideswiped it." I want to apologize to my mom because it was me I love you, Mom. It was me who wrecked your beautiful car.

MJ Night

I would go to the nightclub at Strawberry Square in downtown Harrisburg to dance like Michael Jackson all night. My confidence was through the roof! While the ladies loved it, some of the gentlemen had a problem with it. I remember one night, the uptown gang came in and noticed that I was on the dance floor. There was a particular guy who everyone knew as "Steve". He didn't like me at all because my confidence was growing stronger and there were a lot of women who made it known that they were interested in me. I had a great personality, excellent interaction skills and there was an undertone of my popularity grew from other people in the city. Perhaps from his vantage point, I was a middle-class kid who thought I was better than everyone else but he had no idea, not even my siblings and I knew that we were a struggling middle-class family. My mother and father worked extremely hard to take care of us but to him, I was just an enemy trying to take the shine away from the other guys in the club. In reality, I was just being ME. So this particular evening, Steve saw and wanted to engage in a confrontational battle. I told him to meet me outside. He was with one other person but I didn't care. I walked outside but he ran to bring some more of his friends. His friends didn't come out right away but I walked to the parking lot with my brother Keith based on the fact that they didn't come out right away. I wanted to avoid conflict but they saw me and he started running down the hallway in the back. When I was growing up I watched Bruce Lee movies. I would practice karate moves for hours and I was amazed at my ability to fight just like I saw it in the movies. I knew exactly how I was going to beat his ass. So as he ran towards me, I threw up my leg the way. Just like Bruce Lee would do kicked him to the floor right in the middle of his chest! My enemy was defeated with one swift kick to the chest! His friends stood there totally amazed at me being able to do this to their friend. They probably thought I had additional moves up my sleeve but that's all I had at the time…but they didn't need to know that. But I was a beast at using nun chucks and my Bruce Lee moves were second nature to me. That fight could have gone another way but God planted a seed in me and taught me how to protect myself when my enemy tried to harm me.

My First Love/Becoming Chaseray

One of my first serious relationships, was with a young lady by the name of Remy Brooks We started going to the mall and having downright fun together…until I started drinking too much with my brother or cousins. I would go to her house and spend the night with her while her stepmother worked nights at the hospital. Sometimes I would be so drunk to the point where we'd have sex, and I would jump out of the bed doing foolish things too embarrassing to speak of to this day. I was so intoxicated until I had no idea what I was doing at this point. I would jump right back in the bed and sleep until an hour before her mother came home. I knew it was so wrong …but I am just sharing this with you that we don't know what people have been through in their lives. Things may look great on the outside, but everyone has a story to tell. Your story can help someone else become free from their past mistakes and go forward in freedom. But I digress. My relationship with Remy was also wonderful until she started hanging out with some other girls at the park. She was very sexy, and knew it, so she would go to the park and flirt with other guys. I noticed she enjoyed the attention she was receiving from them. Especially her ex-boyfriend, Chris. I was furious because I kept telling her she needed to stop going to the park while I was working. I've been a hard worker even as a teenager. I worked at Wendy's, KFC and McDonald's…sometimes simultaneously. She refused to stop flirting with these other guys even after I told her that if she didn't stop, I was going to end the relationship. She didn't care, and neither did I at this point. So one day I was at Remy's house sitting on her front porch waiting for her to return from the park. I noticed Jill walking by herself on 17th Street so I ran up to her and asked if it was okay for me to walk home with her. She agreed. I knew that I was attracted to her and wanted to build something with her. Suddenly, I hear Remy yelling my name and asking me what I was doing. I paid no attention to her and kept walking with Jill side by side all the way to her house. Remy meant a lot to me, and we had lots of challenges, but I liked being around her for the most part. Eventually, we realized we both had so much more we wanted to accomplish in life before becoming too serious. We broke things off and I began to spend even more time with Jill.

Before I had the courage to talk to Jill, I remember hanging with my friend, T.P. We used to spend countless hours at his house on the second floor on 18th Street with the windows open smoking marijuana in his room. T.P.'s mom was real cool and she allowed us to smoke in the house. We'd watch friends walk by, including all the different girls walking up and down the street. But we would not be just looking at any girl, we would be looking out the window at the most attractive girl on the block. That girl was Jill and EVERYBODY wanted to date her. As much as I wanted to date her I knew she was TOTALLY out of my league. As time passed, I was able to build up my confidence to talk to her. No one knew I had a crush on her since the third grade...but T.P knew. Jill was one of the most amazing girls I had ever encountered. She was beautiful with an incredible smile with a gap in her teeth. She was breathtaking. I loved this woman more than anything (puppy love) and would do anything for her but her Dad loved her more. We started spending time together after I mustered up the courage to talk to her. I had even more courage to talk to her because Remy wouldn't stop her flirtatious behavior with other guys so I started spending almost all of my time with Jill. I didn't have a car at that time but her Dad had a Cadillac so I rode back-and-forth to college with her. Jill's father would do almost anything for his daughter and I had the privilege of dating her. We would sit in her living room watching TV and listening to El DeBarge, one of her favorite singing groups. One time, she and I were watching a classic movie called, "The Promoter". It was about an entertainment promoter and the making of a star. The promoter's goal was to take a person who was unsuccessful and transform them into a singing sensation. This movie reminded me of my life because he had to prove to his peers that he could be successful and help somebody else win in life that may not have had the same opportunities as others. The promoter noticed this kid and gave him a new name from his original name. That was the beginning of his transformation from ordinary to extraordinary. While watching that movie, that's when I changed my name to "Chaseray" because I was so inspired by this. I had been called Jerome all of my life but I knew I was destined for greatness, so I changed my name. Just like the kid in the movie, I realized that I had an opportunity to move forward with my life and become wildly successful. Just like the kid in the movie, I declared that day that I would go from rags to riches and be somebody great. I told everybody that I no longer will be called Jerome but I will be called Chaseray!

Getting to Know Chaseray

My upbringing groomed me to enjoy the attention that I received from women. Everybody in my circle was doing it, so I thought that was the thing to do, but it was wrong. From age 15 to 21, my life was all about money, going to school and back-to-back sexual encounters with certain types of women. My personality and character were constantly transforming due to attending Bishop McDevitt Catholic School where I had a really great football career. I became one of the most dominant football players as a freshman and sophomore.It was clear that I was destined to be a high school superstar when suddenly my mother could no longer afford for me to continue to go to the school. Sadly, I had to go back to public school where I was enrolled at William Penn High School where my football career ended. I was terrified because the school was uptown which would increase my risk of being exposed to gang violence. I would take the bus uptown, and my best defense was to establish myself like a crazy person. At this point, I was known as "Mad Puppy" among the students because my brother, Curtis was known as "Mad Dog." I went along with the persona that we were gangsters, and I became extremely obnoxious. I was so out of control to the point where people were afraid of me. I would do crazy things like take my head and break out the school bus windows or jump out of the bus exit door and climb on top of the bus. I was even known to run on top of my bus and jump from one bus to another and then jump off! I would be in major trouble since I could've been seriously injured or killed along with putting countless others in harm's way. There were times while at school I would obnoxiously run down the hallways and slide from one end to the other just to be annoying. One time, I even took the Christmas tree and threw it right out the front door! Even at this point, there was a seed in me.

One day while at school, I ran across the notorious uptown gang and they wanted to fight me. Suddenly, they cornered me in the hallway along with a guy named Big Mike. I knew there was no way I could get out of this moment in one piece, so I started acting like Curly from "The Three Stooges" and started violently smacking myself in the face. Then I took my head and crashed it into the nearest window. After that, I turned around and stood in a defensive posture prepared to fight anyone standing in my way. They were completely astonished that I took my head and busted out the window without splitting my brain into shreds, so they turned around and ran like they'd seen a ghost! Big Mike turned to me and said, "You are one crazy motherfucker!" And from that very moment, my reputation at the high school began to soar. No one wanted to mess with me, and I wanted it to stay just like that.

William Penn was considered a co-op school and I was involved in a program called DECA or Distributive Education Clubs of America. DECA was designed to teach high school students sales, advertising, management, and other business skills. I was blessed with the opportunity to learn the art of advertising. Part of the day I would go to my regular classes and then the other part of the day I would attend DECA. After that, I would go to work, so I didn't have to spend that much time at school. Most days I would skip school with Big Mike to hang out with girls, smoke some weed or drink until we were intoxicated or high and then go right back to school. There were many times we'd skip and never come back. To this day I don't know how I made it through school because I struggled academically, but God planted a seed in me!

I remember growing up and drinking Gordon's Gin which was a clever aphrodisiac. It had a reputation for giving the fellas an extreme hard on and making me totally fearless. I remember going to the lunchrooms and jumping on the tables running on top of people's food. After school, you just might find me jumping from the second-floor window down to the ground! During this time I was pretty popular. It all started when my brother Curtis, who was in the U.S. Army came home from Korea and said to me, "Hey, I got a proposition for you." I didn't know any better so he told me for every full bag of weed that I was able to sell he would give me a percentage of the money. So instead of stealing, I would sell weed. I became really good at it and had money to buy more drugs and make even more money. There were times when I would be walking around with wads of cash anywhere from $750 to as much as $1000. I used to go to several bars even at the age of 16. There were a ton of bars in Harrisburg and Steelton. Even though I was underage, I had so much money. I was able to buy my way into any bar or club at any time. Even as a young cat, I was considered a "high roller" because I would buy drinks for everybody in the bar. My popularity in my city continued to increase because most folks knew if I was in the bar I would not hesitate to say, "Drinks on me!"

I loved the bar scene because it was so exciting! That was the proper thing to do back then, and we'd end up hanging out and socializing and checking out the ladies. Two ladies, in particular, were good friends that we started hanging out with. We would talk to them on the phone for long periods of time, but finally, they decided they wanted us to hook up for a double date. Unbeknownst to me, one of the girls I was attracted to had a boyfriend who was a well-known member of a gang. Once I discovered that I immediately I ended the relationship, but Alan continued to date the other lady. My cousin was also a married man. It was not uncommon for The Johnson Brothers to have a wife and a girlfriend. My Uncle Robert and Alan had a wife and so many girlfriends before the Harvey Boys even knew what it was to enjoy the best of both worlds. I was still young and didn't have a wife, but I was enjoying my youth. I didn't realize it at the time, but the seed that was planted in me to excel in business started as a young man who as an excellent street pharmacist learned advertising, distribution, sales, and entertaining people. Even though I was engaging in evil at the time, I was going through intense developmental training for success that I would later achieve in life. It's amazing how God will allow all things, even the bad, to work for our benefit in the end.

Stop the Bullying

As I've shared with you before, I spent a lot of time in my younger days running long distances in Harrisburg Park sometimes up to 5 miles at a time. I would run nonstop which prepared me when I had to run home from Harrisburg Middle School, especially when I was being bullied by five or more people simultaneously. I was never a coward, but in most cases, I was outnumbered and running for my life was my only option. I learned a very valuable lesson over the years, and that is when you are outnumbered. No one should be fighting, it's a losing battle, and it's time to RUN! I was constantly being bullied, and people did their best to try to intimidate me. Even though I felt scared at times, acting scared was not an option! As I grew older, the people who bullied me started running from me. I made up in my mind that if I ever saw the people who bullied me, I would not make them pay for what they did to me even though I had every right to do it. I could not tell my brothers because it would have made the situation worse down the road.

There is a still, small, internal voice that will always show you a better way of living, doing and being. As you can see in my story, God always showed me the way and provided a way of escape out of some of the situations I found myself in. I remember the summer after I graduated from high school, I was walking down Market Street, and I saw my number one bully, Steve, from when I was in the eighth grade. He was in the ninth grade and was always in and out of jail throughout his childhood. As I was walking toward him, I could feel the anger and frustration take over me as I briefly reflected on the HELL he put me through. When he realized who I was, he immediately turned around and hauled ass down Market street! I chased him and almost caught him. I yelled, "NOW, you know how it feels!!" I felt victorious at that moment because I didn't allow my number one bully to beat me this time! I finally conquered my fear, and I told him exactly what was on my mind! I yelled some other expletives, but I knew I could not do to him what he had done to me and so many other people. STOP THE BULLYING!

It's not enough to constantly complain about what's wrong with your life, but it's time for you to do something about it!

4

Whatever You Want,
Put It in the Hat

IT WAS JULY 10, 1984, and I had a hunger to achieve MORE in life. I had to make a decision whether to move away from home to have a better life or remain in familiar territory and bang my head against the glass ceiling of the environment I grew up in. At first, I was afraid to make up my mind to go or stay. Finally, I said to myself, "I can't take this anymore!" All of my life, people would tell me that I couldn't do this or that. From teachers to bosses, even some friends and family, they said I would never accomplish anything in life. Being called, "stupid" was normal for me, but I just didn't care about any of that. I didn't care what the naysayers thought I could accomplish. I KNEW God planted a seed in me and I had to do something about it. I knew I was not created to be "status quo" or average, but I was called by God to be EXTRAORDINARY, and my purpose in life was to help others become extraordinary as well. At some point, I realized that whatever I wanted, I had to put it in the atmosphere. Wishing upon a star is nice, but you won't reach your goals simply wishing something will come to pass. It's not enough to constantly complain about what's wrong with your life, but it's time for you to do something about it! Do you know a person like this? Whatever you want, put it in the hat. The hat represents the universe. You have to speak to the universe and tell it exactly what you want from it. I became determined enough to not just long for a better life but to CREATE one. How do you live a great life? You must be FEARLESS! How do you put food on the table to feed your family? You must be a BELIEVER! How do you obtain a promotion to the next level of your job? You must be FEARLESS! Are you FED UP enough to tell the universe what you want or do you want to spend more time complaining about the past? What do you do when you want to get in shape? You must be hungry for the RIGHT food to put in your body and exercise at least 2-3 times a week. You know what that's called? Discipline! You must be hungry for D I S C I P L I N E. You have to discipline your mouth to say only those things that will benefit your future. What do you need to do to purchase your dream house? You must see the invisible as possible! Take a few seconds, no matter where you are reading this and say, **"I was born to fulfill God's purpose. This is why He planted the seed in me!"** I don't care what you want to accomplish you MUST be so ready to fulfill your destiny.

Moving Day

I had been working in Harrisburg at a variety of different jobs. Between the Noodle Factory, Berg Electronics, and IBM I was making about $17.00 per hour. I would see on TV that Houston was booming economically. My cousins Tony and Vickie had relocated to Houston a couple of years prior and I knew it was time for me to make a move. It was now or never! I told my mom a week before I left that I was moving from Harrisburg to Houston to start my new life. I was serious about making this move. I gave both of my cars to my brothers because I knew I would not be back. As Anthony Robbins stated, "You have to burn the boats" that way there is no turning back. Now it's moving day and my mother was so upset because she didn't want me to leave. She called her older brother, Robert over to the house to stop me. When he arrived, my Mom and I were standing in the living room as I was about to head to the airport. My uncle asked me one question, "Boy, have you ever been on an airplane before?" I said, "No, Sir." He said, "Evelyn, he will be back. As soon as he lands in Houston, he'll be taking the next airplane back home." I kissed my mother goodbye and off I went to the airport. I was totally amazed once I arrived to the airport and that what I was doing was for real. I boarded the airplane and the door shut. Suddenly, everything became even more real. Would you know that my uncle was right? From the time the airplane took off, I cried like a baby missing my mom, sister, and brothers. I was on my way to another part of the planet! I couldn't wait for the plane to land in Houston. As the airplane started to descend, I was scared and excited to take the next plane home. Once the plane landed, I rushed to the ticket counter to buy a return flight home. The ticket agent was ready to take my money but suddenly, I stopped. Before I gave her the money I started thinking about what my uncle said I would do. The ticket agent said, "Are you ready to pay?" I said, "No." She said, "Why?" I replied, "Because my Uncle Robert told me I would do this very thing after my first airplane ride away from home and that I would run back home to mommy." He told me I wasn't going to amount to anything and I would be back. I want to thank Uncle Robert because little did I know that what he had done for me was change my life in a major way. I vowed to stay in Houston and prove him and everybody else wrong. I am going to show the world what I was capable of.

I went to baggage claim where my cousins, Tony and Vickie were waiting for me. Back in New Jersey at their relocation party, I asked if I could move to Houston with them. They said, "Yes." and I was shocked. After two years had passed, I ask again, and they said, "Yes" but the rule was I had to secure my own place within 30 days. Wow! This was "Motivation 101," and it lit a fire under me. It ended up taking a little longer than that, and they graciously extended the time to 90 more days. God knows who to put in your life at the right time. Tony and Vickie helped me secure a car and an apartment plus so many other things. They gave me a roof over my head, food, love, and a family with cousins, Doug, Victor, and Andre along with Vickie's sister, Velda.

Tony and I were always working on special projects around the house. One time we decided to install a sprinkler system and ended up cutting a major gas line to the house. We almost blew up the house…LOL! I will always remember, "The Retreat Room" which was my favorite room for relaxation at their beautiful home. I used to say to myself, "I can't wait to have one of those one day!" Frankly, they showed me in an up-close and personal way how a loving family works from the inside. Tony and Vickie are two remarkable people that knew their roles as husband and wife very well. They made a lasting impression on me. One of the reasons I have a fantastic family life today is because of the excellent example Tony and Vickie set for me. They are incredible.

The Borrowed Car

My cousins gave me first-class treatment. They even allowed me to use their car so that I could find a job. One day, I finally secured a job at a shoe store, and I was so excited! When I was driving down Highway 59 in Houston and not paying attention, I ran Tony and Vickie's Nissan in the back of another car. I in myself, and I just knew they were going to be real mad at me. So when I arrived home they asked me was I ok which was more important than the car. This blew me away. They cared about me more than their car. Are you kidding me right now? This shows exactly how amazing they are. I am grateful to have a family of this caliber. Most families are not like this, but God placed me in this family to learn what I needed to know; how to be a great family man.

Times Up!

My last day at Tony and Vickie's finally came...times up! Tony helped me find a Cadillac Coupe Deville with a gold and off-white vinyl top. I was the man!! I was moving to Woodlake Apartments, but this was a day full of mixed emotions. This was a big step, moving out on my own. They gave me a box spring bed with two planks. It would sink in the middle when I laid on it, but I was still grateful. They also gave me a black and white TV that worked for a short period but then the picture went out. After a while, it only had sound, but no picture. I packed up the car and Tony said, "Goodbye and good luck." I shut the door and immediately started crying because finally, I'm really all on my own. I was working at Sharpstown Mall at a shoe store making $4.25 an hour plus commissions. Money was super tight, so every day for the next year I went to work and right back home. I didn't even go to the barbershop, so I just let my hair grow. On Sunday nights during the winter months, I worked outside the Circle K convenience store waiting for people to buy logs for their fireplace. I helped them put the logs in their trunk for tips. Thursday nights was ladies' night at one of the local clubs so I would go during happy hour and guys paid a $5.00 cover charge. I wore this really nice red dress jacket where I sewed four zip locks bags into the pockets. My mom taught us how to sew as kids, and this was a pivotal moment where that skill came in handy! So I had "all you can eat" ham and chicken in one bag, the bread and cheese into another pocket and the veggies in another pocket. For the rest of the night I would enjoy the entertainment, but then I would go home and put those "sew-ins" in the refrigerator. This would pretty much be my lunch for the following week. On Fridays, I would go and pick up government cheese and powdered milk. So this was how I survived for an entire year until I could afford to buy more groceries. I was used to doing this because back home when one of my parents was out of work we had to do that for years growing up as a kid. Also, I remember the gas shortage. You could only buy gas on certain days. If you had an even number, you could buy gas on Tuesdays and Thursdays. If you had an odd number, you could buy gas on Mondays and Wednesdays. It was a tough time for everyone. Some people would switch license plates with other people just to secure more gas. I had to do what I had to do, and I knew how to survive. Thank you, Mom and Dad.

I lived like a homeless person in my apartment. I stopped having my hair cut on a weekly basis because I was living paycheck to paycheck. I was making $4.25 plus commission which came out to be about $300 a week after taxes. After I had been in Houston a while, my older brother, Keith came to visit me for the very first time. He was instrumental in helping me build my confidence. He helped me put my life back on track. He noticed I hadn't been to the barbershop in a while and he said, "Man, what are you doing? Why didn't you cut your hair and groom yourself right?" I said, "Well, I don't have any money after paying bills." He said, **"Hey, man, before anything, always make sure you take care of yourself."** That's when I started going back to the barbershop and redefining myself. That was very important advice my brother gave me because I was still very homesick and crying from time to time. A lot of people didn't know I was very depressed. My brother told me, "Chaseray, things will start happening for you if you start believing in yourself again just like you did in Harrisburg." Lo and behold, it did! I became promoted to store manager at Westwood Mall! See? No one can hold you back but yourself. The store manager working for the shoe store tried to hold me back. Even after calling me a nigger, God still created an amazing path for me. My team and I did an outstanding job with my first store.

> *"Teamwork is the ability to work together toward a common vision. It is the fuel that allows common people to attain uncommon results."* - *Andrew Carnegie*

I've been through so many things since I've been in Houston. Mentally those challenges afforded me the opportunity to grow up. **I would like to let you know that when you are growing up, and you face adversity, there is going to be a lot of people out there trying to stop you.** I had so many people demoralize and humiliate me. Therefore, I would break out in hives and even have anxiety and panic attacks. Sometimes I would have heart palpitations and a variety of different physical things when I would deal with verbal abuse and discrimination. There is a list of things that you go through physically and mentally when people put you through hell. Through it all, the negativity helped me to be successful later in life. I was able to endure many hardships at a young age. As a young boy, that's when I learned that when anybody told me that I could not do something that was the thing that motivated me the most to prove them wrong.

The power inside of us that's been given by God is unlimited. We are His creation, and we must understand there are no limits until you allow someone to set limits of fear and emotional anguish inside of you. The naysayers create limits which can cause anxiety, however, keep calm and understand that there are no true limits to accomplishing things as long as it's done right. There's unlimited power inside you that God has given you.

A One-Woman Man

It was 1988 when my career started to skyrocket in the men's fashion industry. I began to obtain notoriety within the company due to my contagious personality and unorthodox management style. The senior leaders allowed me to write motivational articles in the company newsletter. My picture would also be featured with the article, so the entire company knew who I was even if I didn't know who they were. One of my colleagues, Kim, was in charge of training for the Texas and Louisiana markets. One day, she was doing a routine visit to the Baton Rouge, Louisiana location and came across a young lady by the name of Mattie. She had to be about 17 at the time and was seemingly quite smitten with me (smile). When Kim returned back to Houston, she told me this young lady thought I was cute and I should give her a call. I immediately rejected the idea of calling her because first of all, I am not into long-distance relationships and secondly I don't know her like that to just up and call her. No, thank you! I blew it off, and we never spoke of her again. About five years later, I became Regional Manager responsible for the Louisiana market, and it was time for a visit. There were some promotions that needed to be made, and Mattie Ricard name came up on my list. I knew the name sounded familiar, but I had honestly forgotten what Mattie shared with Kim about me. I held up the promotions until I could really grasp the climate of the market. Apparently, Mattie became quite frustrated, so she called me and wanted to know what the holdup was. She said, "I was promised a promotion, and it was explained to me that YOU are the reason I have not been promoted yet." I smiled to myself before responding because I could feel how upset she was through the phone. I remained calm and replied, "I appreciate your call, Mattie, however, I am still conducting assessments of the entire market which is causing the delay. As soon as I have completed my assessments, a decision will be made." I could feel her disappointment as she hung up but I knew she'd be okay. A week later she was promoted to Stylist. Mattie was masterful at styling, and the customers trusted her judgment. The first real interaction I had with her was quite vivid. She had just closed a $2000.00 sale, and she was very excited about it. She walked over to me and said, "So what did you think about that sale?" I told her, "It was fantastic! Your service to the client was unbelievable, and your selling techniques were phenomenal. Are you open to more coaching?" "Yes." Then I asked her, "What do you think could have made that sale better?" She paused for a moment to process my question and then replied, "I don't know. What do you think?" I replied, "Well if you weren't chewing gum then it would've been PERFECT!" She went OFF! She began to voice her frustration and her dislike for me. I can't remember exactly what she said to me, but I do know she was visibly upset and did everything in her power to AVOID me at all costs. The thing is, I ASKED her if she was open to coaching and I guess she just wasn't ready at the time.

As time progressed, there were three other ladies on the team at the Baton Rouge location. They wanted to know what type of man I was. They even placed a bet on who would have the opportunity to have a relationship with me first. These women were strategic and persistent. They tried every tactic they could from being overly kind to flat out persuasion and negotiation. I had never been winked at so much in my life. From tight-fitting dresses to making passes at me, they were ruthless and wanted to win. I didn't dare to even make an attempt to be involved with any of them. There was a time I probably would have entertained all of them simultaneously but I had been transformed. I was a changed man with morals, standards, and values. I was not interested in jeopardizing my career to have an exchange with these women. At the age of 23, I decided that I would never disrespect another woman again. I was no longer interested in disrespecting myself or my mother ever again. Even though these ladies pranced and paraded around me to attempt to seduce me, I stood my ground. Things became so out of control to the point that when the company had store visits or holiday functions, they would try to find the hotel room I was staying in to try to seduce me. There was a company event in New Orleans and there was a young lady by the name of Tee who was insistent upon seducing me. Somehow she found out what room I was in and knocked on my door. I could see through the peephole who it was even though I asked who it was because I knew I was NOT going to open that door! I asked her through the door, "What do you need?" She was clearly annoyed and she said, "Come on, just open the door!" I slowly opened the door and she was standing there with a trench coat and black pumps. She then opens the coat and she was totally naked. I froze for a hot second but I quickly snapped out of it. I told her, "I'm truly flattered but no, thank you!" She hollered back, "Are you GAY!?" I said, "No, but I am not the type of guy." Now, don't misunderstand me, it was tempting and she was quite appealing, but I was just no longer in that place. I refused to go back to the man I used to be. I was ready to be a one-woman man. I have always attracted this type of attention throughout my entire career. I was now able to activate the superpower of discipline my father taught me as a kid. Trust me it was difficult to say, "No" but I knew God planted a seed in me and I needed to see it come to fruition by staying focused on my goals.

Love for a Lifetime

A couple of visits had gone by since Mattie became upset with me due to the feedback I shared about her sales performance. She slowly starting talking to me again and eventually, things went back to normal. We had become really good co-workers, and there was never anything romantic between us. When I would visit the store even though she was a hard worker she was able to have fun during the slow times. We would crack jokes, laugh and had fun with the entire staff.

Mattie had just graduated from Southern University, and she was engaged to be married to an NFL football player. One day after a store visit, I was about to leave, and I asked Mattie what she had planned for the weekend. She told me she was headed to Chicago. Ironically, I was going to the same city to see the Chicago Bears play the Houston Oilers with my friend, Robert. Robert and I were going to a party and then to the game on Sunday with some other friends of ours. Coincidentally, Mattie tells me she was also going to see her fiancé play in the game. So once we arrived in Chicago, we called Mattie to come hang with us because we all work together at the same company. The Chicago Fashion Team was hosting a party at his apartment, so we picked her up from her fiancé's apartment. When she was headed towards the car, one of my friends told me he was going hit on her, and I told him, "No Way! She has a fiancé." But that didn't stop him! So we went to the party and had a great time until 2am. It became too late to drive Mattie back to her fiancé's apartment, so she called him and let him know she was staying with us and that she was ok. My friend believed this was his opportunity once we arrived back to his apartment to hit on her. This was a one bedroom apartment, and my friend was going to make his move on her once the rest of us fell asleep. I told him, "No Way! Over my dead body!" Mattie never knew what was going on and to make sure nothing happened I slept on the floor outside the bedroom she was sleeping in to make sure of it! Her fiancé trusted us, and I wasn't going to let my friend mess it up for us. A couple of months later, Mattie invited me to the engagement party. I flew in that week with Karen to attend the party. Unknown to Mattie, I came with Karen so I called her to ask if it was ok for another co-worker could come with me. She said no due to seating. I let her know that it was ok, but I would not be attending because Karen was going to be stuck out there alone. So while on the phone, Mattie asked her Mom if it was okay to bring the co-worker in which she said it was okay. Mattie still wanted her mom to say "no," but she said, "yes" anyway. At the time, this seemed very suspicious to me, but I didn't ask her why. I just moved on and was happy Karen was able to come to the engagement party.

I was honored to be a part of the event, and it was amazing. Once we arrived to the event, Mattie's mother grabbed me by the hand and took me around to everyone at the party. She introduced me to every single person at the event which I also found awfully unusual. I overlooked it because this was the south. I learned it was traditional hometown behavior to call everyone, "Baby." At first, I thought everyone was hitting on me, but later I noticed every lady said it. It is considered a high level of respect for the people they are talking to.

About six months later, it was time for the wedding. I went to the Baton Rouge, Louisiana location to cover so the staff could attend the wedding. A few minutes later, Mattie shows up to work. I am shocked that she is standing there and I say, "Hey...wait one second. You are supposed to be getting married today!" She says, "No, I'm not getting married anymore." I did my best to encourage her by saying, "Well, sometimes people break up to make up you will get back together I know it." I could tell she was truly done with the relationship when she said, "No, not this time. It will not happen. It's over!" So then I said to her, "Ok, well if you want to make yourself available for other people you have to take that 4-carat ring off." She walked away and started working. So the next day, she came to work, and I noticed she didn't have the ring on. I was shocked she took my advice. She actually took the ring off. I was there with my colleague, Karen to help cover the store because it was Mattie's wedding day, but she decided not to get married. She didn't inform us beforehand because had we known we wouldn't have come. When it was time to leave, I didn't say anything to anyone about Mattie taking off the ring. Once Karen and I said our goodbyes to everyone, once we sat in the car; I said, "Hey, I have something to tell you." She said, "Chaseray, I already know you are in love with Mattie." I said, "Who? Really? Mattie? You think so?" She said, "Yes, need to stop playing around. I notice how you both light up when are in the presence of each other. I believe a man should always be a true gentleman to everyone, but she was right. I really cared very deeply for Mattie, but I always kept my distance because I knew she had a fiancé who I had great respect for. Plus, I did not believe in dating co-workers. Karen told me, "Well, you need to tell her your feelings. I believe she feels the same way about you." I thought about everything on the flight back to Houston and finally mustered up enough courage to call Mattie. I honestly didn't know what to expect or how she would respond. I said, "Hey, I have something to tell you." She replied, "I have something to tell you, too." We decided to wait until we saw each other face-to-face before sharing.

About five weeks later, Kim and I went back to Baton Rouge for another visit. That evening, Mattie met up with us for dinner. We all had great food and conversation which ran late into the night. Since Mattie lived about 45 minutes away, it was too late to drive home. I suggested, "Why not stay with Kim in her room and go home in the morning? Plus, we can tell each other what we want to say to each other." Mattie said, "Yes." The three of us went back to the hotel and started watching TV and engaging in great conversation. Eventually, Kim ended up falling asleep. That was the moment we realized we were in love with one another. Mattie said, "I have something to tell you: I thought you were dating Kim." I said, "No way. She's like a sister to me, and she is head over heels madly in love with my business partner, The Italian Stallion!" Mattie admitted, "That's why I didn't want her to come to the engagement party." We continued to have a great conversation...beating around the bush on what we really wanted to say to each other.

So she said, "Ok, I have something else to tell you, but you go first on what you wanted to say to me." I said, "Ok let's both say it on the count of three...1...2..3..... "I love you!!!" Immediately, we started kissing each other and never stopped kissing. We were sitting on the bed but then we rolled on to the floor. We were wrapped in the blanket with our clothes on still kissing. (Kim was still asleep the whole time.)

We finally stood up after kissing on the floor for two more hours straight. We looked at each other and started kissing again. We went into the bathroom at 4 am and continued kissing non-stop until 5 am. We stopped because we both had to go to work a few hours later. Mattie decided it was time to say, "good night" or morning (smile).

As we stood outside of Karen's hotel room, we started kissing again, but the door closed on us. Mattie accidentally left her key in the room with Karen, so we went to my room. As soon as we arrived, we started kissing again with our clothes still on from 5 am to 8 am. We finally stopped in total disbelief of what just happened. We started talking about things leading up to this amazing moment for both of us. Mattie reflected on how she noticed my picture in the company newspaper and thought I was cute, but realized she really didn't like me after our first in-person encounter. She mentioned the first voicemail I left her that she listened to with her mother. Even though she was with someone else at the time, she started having feelings for me. She talked about the prayer meeting led by Pastor Walter at her home. As they were praying, he invited everyone in attendance to put whatever they wanted in the hat. This prayer meeting was six months prior to our moment of confessing our love for one another. Mattie put my business card into the hat, and now here we are. Deeply and passionately in love. Now, this may seem unorthodox to some people, but she had faith that one day we would be together even when I didn't. Six months later, her faith move became her reality. She talked about the picnic and events we attended and how I threw water on her, her mother, Gloriastine, and her Aunt Betty. All of these moments were very special. With all of that being said, I made a major decision in a very short period of time to marry her. Ever since that day, Mattie and I spoke consistently every second of the day and all night. We truly enjoyed one another. I told her I was coming to see her in Louisiana.

I knew I didn't want to be engaged for a long time. I was the consummate professional, and I did not believe in having relationships with women who I worked with. I wouldn't even be seen in a photo with a woman because I wanted to maintain those healthy boundaries. But Mattie was special, and I knew I had to make her my wife. Three weeks later, it was a Tuesday which happened to be the Fourth of July I asked her father and mother for her hand in marriage to be my wife. I put a ring on her finger and her toe. Yes, her toe. I wanted all of Mattie to marry me. It was truly magical and monumental moment for both of us. I even asked the owner of the company and the senior leaders for their blessing to marry this woman because I was in love with her. I wanted to do everything right this time. I wanted to spend the rest of my life with her and beyond because I loved her. She was such an incredible person, and I wanted to make her mine. I know Mattie was a gift from God because she was 23 and I was 35 at the time and her parents allowed me to marry her. Mattie's mom knew all along how much Mattie loved me, and I didn't really know that, but later learned just how much she truly loved me.

One day while on another visit to Baton Rouge, Mattie said that she wanted to take me out for a night on the town. She insisted on coming to pick me up from the hotel, so I waited patiently for her arrival. I stepped off the elevator and immediately noticed a very distinguished gentleman. He was older but very stately and mature. Wisdom was all over this man, and I just kept staring at him. As I walked closer, I realized it was Eddie Robinson, the world-renowned football coach of Grambling State University. I was totally amazed to meet this gentleman while on my way to my first official date with my future wife. I asked him for an autograph, and I didn't know at that time but understand now how monumental that moment was and the day was just beginning. A few moments later, a young man came to me and asked, "Are you Chaseray Harvey?" "Yes, I am." He replied, "Someone's outside waiting for you." I follow the young man through the lobby to the front entrance and there is a beautiful white stretch limousine. The young man said, "The person is inside." He opens the door, and there she is. The most magnificent woman God ever created, My Mattie. She was sitting in the back looking absolutely stunning. We embraced each other and exchanged passionate kisses as we drove around the city of Baton Rouge taking pictures and just loving on each other. The limousine driver took us to the most beautiful parts of the city especially around the ponds and lakes where it was so beautiful to witness. We were riding around listening to Toni Braxton's first CD. The driver was gracious enough to keep playing the music over and over again. We enjoyed an amazing dinner at Ruth Chris and then headed back to the hotel. We exchanged one final kiss along with an embrace and then she departed. It was such a magical, Cinderella moment. The limousine was our chariot for the evening, and Mattie looked absolutely breathtaking. I can remember exactly what she was wearing. A beautiful short, gray skirt set and she had a short, bob haircut with red lipstick.

I could still smell her scent once I returned to my room. I was wearing a black and white double-breasted plaid suit. This was probably one of the best days of my life to this day. The weather was perfect…about 75 degrees. Not only did I have the chance of a lifetime to meet one of the world's most beloved football coaches but I had the opportunity to spend the day with the woman I would spend a lifetime with. That night, we decided to marry three months later. My wife's ex-boyfriends still call to check on us at least once per month. These gentlemen always hoped I would mess up my relationship with Mattie. That is not going to happen because when God ordains something, no one can stop it. When you have faith, it can move mountains you didn't even realize were there.

Heart's Desire

Have you ever had a desire but was too afraid to say it out loud in fear it may not come to pass? One day my brother-in-law, Frank and I were talking about our dreams, goals, and desires. At the time I was living in a modest home, but desired more for my family. While sitting in the backyard entertaining family and friends, I looked Frank in the eye I said, "I am gonna live in a home five times the value of this home one of these days. I don't know how I am going to do it, but it's going to happen!" Remember, whatever you want, PUT IT IN THE HAT! Once you say what you want, then discipline yourself to properly prepare for what you want. Needless to say, my family and I are residing in that home today. There were a variety of God moments that took place leading up to moving into the house. The bank told me I didn't have enough credit to secure the home. I told them I have God, and I believe in Him, and He will make a way. A few days later, they called me back and said we were approved! Your words are a seed and whatever you say has the power to come to pass.

    I desired so many things for my family to enjoy like a basketball court and an outdoor kitchen with a bathroom as well as other things for our new home. Once I told God the desires of my heart, everything changed quickly and drastically! We secured our new home, but we still needed carpenters, plumbers, and bricklayers to finish certain projects. With God being at the center of our life, He allowed us to do so many things that were totally incredible. As I stated earlier, another God moment was after we purchased the house we wanted to have an outdoor kitchen and basketball court built, but it was going to cost us approximately $35,000+. I took a step back, prayed about it and put it in God's hands. When it was all said and done, it only ended up costing us $3000. This is how it happened: when we moved to a new subdivision, I saw a contractor framing a new house. I asked him if he would do the framing for our outdoor kitchen with a bathroom at my house. He told me, "Yes, for $1000." When the plumber showed up to put the plumbing in for the new house next door to me, I asked him if he would run the plumbing for my outdoor bathroom. He said, "Yes, for $500." The gas grill, sink, and bathroom only cost $1500. God showed me favor once again.

Another magnificent moment was when I wanted to sell my truck, but my wife promised to sell it to A.I., a young man at her birthday party. After selling it, I started missing how much I used it for "handyman" stuff. So I kept telling my wife how much I missed my truck. She told me to stop worrying about it, and God would bless us. I knew that God had another plan for me because my wife insisted that we sell the truck to A.I. I really missed that truck, and I desired to obtain another one just like it. Two weeks later, we were driving down Barker Cypress Road and lo and behold, I saw the exact same truck, but it was the latest model, a 2005 and mine was a 2000. I ended up buying that truck which I still own to this day. There are so many magnificent things that God continues to do in my life, and He wants to do the same thing in yours. I am so blessed to have an amazing wife, remarkable children as well as relationships that I have with so many outstanding people. I know for some of you that may seem a bit shallow, but I am telling you these stories because I want you not only to dream big but SAY SOMETHING BIG! God continues to provide and do certain things for those who demonstrate extraordinary faith.

Here's what I need you to understand; no one is responsible for the things you put in your hat but YOU! It may take 1,000 attempts or more to achieve your dreams, but you must believe! Putting things in the hat is not just for you to prosper, but for others to see that they, too, can achieve every dream, goal or desire they have ever had if they would just put it in the hat! I want to thank my amazing wife Mattie for making me a believer. Once she came into my life, everything accelerated in my life...I mean EVERYTHING!

When fear or doubt tries to creep into our lives, we take a moment to reflect on our wins, celebrate the learning opportunities and look forward to our winning future.

5

A Whole 'Notha Level

ALLOW ME TO reflect back to when I was about 17 years old when I decided it was time to start refining myself and move from the hustle game to Corporate America. It was time for me to go to a whole 'notha level in my life. Other than the summer jobs that I had that lasted for three months, I never had a job during the entire year until I had the opportunity to work for a shoe store in Harrisburg. The shoe store is where I learned how to transfer the hustle game behavior of selling to selling ladies' shoes, handbags, pantyhose, and heel-plates for the commission. This would allow me to also dress in a professional way with a suit, shirt, and tie. Also, I had the opportunity to serve some of the most beautiful ladies in the entire city. YES! Women love new shoes!! Even though the money was extremely less, it was just a cleaner way to make money and become a better person. When I moved into Corporate America, I was afforded the opportunity to learn other skill sets such as customer service, communication, goal setting, recognition, and working as a team. After working at the shoe store for a while, I moved to the foodservice industry working at McDonald's, Wendy's and KFC learning how to prepare food in addition to what my mother had shown me. My mother taught us how to cook, braid hair, keep house, sew and wash clothes. My mother would always say, "After you learn these skills, you would never need a woman in your life that you would have to depend on her doing these things. You would become a value to her knowing these things, and she will appreciate the value you could bring to the relationship. Boy, was she so right. The weight and stress on most families are when only one person is doing most of the work. **All parents, hear me:** teach your children how to multitask in these areas to allow them to have a richer relationship later in life. Thanks, Mom and Dad for doing it for my brothers and me. My father taught us how to paint, cut grass, work on cars and any type of handyman job. My father set the example. I took the skills that I learned from my parents and those jobs I had as a young man to not only refine myself, but took it to a WHOLE 'NOTHA LEVEL!

I Found My Passion

The first year of my career was amazing but it came with many challenges. I had so much passion for the clothing industry and in that, there was nothing that I would not do to ensure that I performed well in everything I did. Even though I worked hard, never missed a day and stayed focused, the store manager wanted to fire me after only two weeks. During our first interview, the store manager took me into his office and shut the door. He started asking me questions about myself and every time I would respond, someone would hit the door really hard time after time. I asked the store manager did he want to answer the door but he said, "No". That very day I knew I was not wanted there. Houston was a racially charged city at the time and I knew the slamming on the door was nothing but an act of intimidation but I was determined to succeed. I asked for an opportunity to succeed. Reluctantly, the store manager hired me. Two weeks later, I started my first day! I walked in wearing the suit I wore to my high school graduation. The store manager threw a tape measure at me and told me to get to work. I had never used a tape measure before so I had no idea how to use it. I knew it measured things but I didn't know how to measure anybody. As the store opens, the first customer walks in and I greet him by saying, "Thank you for coming. Is there anything I can help you with?" The customer ignores me and walks away. The store manager says to me, "What are you doing?" I said, "I don't really know this job. Somebody needs to train me." I knew the store manager was looking forward to me failing because he kept putting me through these frivolous tasks but God sent me some help. There was an Assistant Manager, who we called B.G., who said, "Chaseray, I will train you. Whenever I work my shifts I will show you what to do." And he did just that. He helped me and showed me exactly what to do. He was a great gentleman and a good person who showed me how the system worked.

The store manager continued to antagonize me a couple of weeks later by saying, "Well, it doesn't seem like you are going to make it." I said, "What do you mean? I think I am doing better than the guy who quit the week before I started. He was averaging $5000.00 in sales a week and I was averaging $6000.00 my first week." He said, "Never mind what that guy did. You're not going to make it in the company and you coming here is bringing down my results!" The second week I was there I generated $7000.00 in sales but he still wasn't satisfied. He said, "You're not going to make it and I have already called the President of the company and told him that I want you gone. And by the way, the Regional Manager is coming today to move you from the store." I said, "Man, I've only been here for two weeks. Please, Sir...just give me a chance!" He said, "No! You need to call your old company back and ask for your job back." Immediately I became so full and I just started crying. So I dropped to my knees and begged and said, "Please give me a chance to stay in this store." And he looked down at me and said, "You are officially being removed!" then he walked away. I was devastated because I had left the shoe store as a store manager to become a Manager-in-Training for this fashion brand. I was willing to start from the bottom to make it to the top. I reflected on how four years prior I was told to get more experience in retail and I did that. Now I am here and I am being set up for failure? I was at the number one store in the city and was doing well for a person with no experience in the fashion business. I pulled myself together when moments later, the Regional Manager came in and told me he was taking me to lunch...his treat. We arrived to the seafood restaurant right across the street and the server immediately seated us. He says to me, "I'm sorry you have to move on but before you do that, I have another option for you. There is a new store in Southwest Houston and if you want that opportunity, you can go there." I knew I could not turn back so then I replied, "I'll take the opportunity." So as we finish eating and I am pulling myself together, he touches his back pocket and says, "Oh, I left my wallet. You're going to have to pay for lunch but I'll pay you back." Even though he promised to pay me back, I was so disappointed in the company and how they treated me. I was given the choice to quit my job or move to this other store but instead of complaining, I went to the other store.

My first day at the new location was quite interesting to say the least. In the company, that team was known as, "The Team of Misfits". Imagine this: we had "The Professor" of the team who knew everything there was to know about the company. Then there was the drop dead gorgeous "Blonde Bombshell" who was the mama bear of the team. Every team has a person who does everything by the book but he was quite interesting. Then there was the store manager, the self-proclaimed "Cowboy" who greeted me when I arrived the first day. He told me, "All you have to do is your job and you will be okay. The Assistant Manager will be in shortly." About 10 minutes later in walks the loudest, most flamboyant guy I had ever seen. The guy we called, "J.H." had on pink socks and had the most contagious attitude of all time. I immediately admired his personality and eventually I almost emulated him because he was truly a force to be reckoned with. He wore the cufflinks with the suspenders and his suits were always well fitted. He had waves in his hair and a greyhound pin on his suit jacket. So he comes over to me in this loud, boisterous voice saying, "Hey, there...I'm J.H.! I see you didn't make it over there at the flagship store but that's okay. They are a bunch of hypocrites at that store and I ain't got time to be training you so just do as I do! And if you can do it, do it better! I'll see you at the finish line, Mister. But if you get there before me, which I doubt, just know that second place is WIDE open for you! Alright, you got it?" I said, "Yea, I got it. " In my mind, I was like, "Who's this guy??" but I immediately felt at home. He told me that I would fit right in with the rest of the team and he was right! That was the motivation I needed and the opportunity I desired to go to another level. I followed J.H.'s lead and within five months, I was number three in the city for the year. I sold over $600,000 in sales in 5 ½ months stemming from doing a variety of different things. One of the things I did was provide a high level of customer service along with a creative and extraordinary team. We specialized in creating raving fans and repeat business. I was selling between $17,000 and $25,000 a week at $5.00 per hour and 3% commission, which at that time, was a substantial amount of money. I was proud of myself and in my excitement because of my accomplishments, I managed to outsell the number one salesperson in the company the very next year. I did exactly what I had planned to do. The President of the company called me and asked, "HOW THE HELL DID YOU DO IT?" I told him I did exactly what J.H. did. The President told the store manager from the old store, "Man, you let go of a Game Changer from your store." His reply was, "Oh, that was just beginner's luck." I told him with the President standing right next to him at the company holiday party, "Next year, I will be the number one salesperson in the entire company!" And I did just that! The next year I won *Salesman of The Year!* My first store manager did not believe in me but God did.

The Set Up...

At this point, I was unstoppable! The upper management was impressed with my performance, but they still weren't convinced that I was really cut out for the business. My Regional Manager told me he wanted to promote me and send me to another store, but it really wasn't going to be a promotion because it was not performing as well. Everyone knew if anyone went to this particular store it would be career suicide. He went on for days asking me to go, and I kept telling him, "No, I'm staying here! We're on track to meet our goal. We took this store from a One Million Dollar store to a $1.5 million store in one year, and I believe we can take it on to a $2,000,000 store in the following year. I am not leaving unless the President calls me!" Can you believe the same guy who stuck me with the lunch bill wanted me to do him a favor? The next day, the President called me and said, "Chas, we need you to go to this other store." I told him, "Only if you all agree to my terms." And I told him what I wanted from a compensation perspective along with a few other things. Upper management agreed to my terms and I decided to take the position because they compensated me well enough to go there based on what I was earning at the time. It was imperative that I properly negotiated this deal if I was going to leave my Assistant Manager position I obtained only after eight months of being with the company to becoming a store manager of a $500,000 store. I also agreed to move to the store if they agreed to my business plan. I told them I needed the right people and merchandise to support turning the store around.

After accepting the position, I went to my first quarterly meeting. It was company tradition to ask the store managers to write down our projections of what the store would generate in sales. I took that same philosophy to the new store. Since I was the new manager, I knew I had something to prove. The first year the store was open the team generated $300,000 in sales over the past 6 years. The best year they generated $500,000. Upper Management wanted to know what we could do now that I was in charge. I confidently expressed to them we would do $1,000,000 million in sales. Immediately, they thought I was crazy and I was putting too much pressure on myself and the staff. They all laughed at me at the meeting due to me being the rookie. The President went so far as to say to me that my sales goals were, "like taking shit and throwing it into a fan". In other words, this was going to backfire on me and I was going to be the laughing stock of the company. The entire up line management team rejected my sales projection and told me I needed to resend a more realistic number and if I didn't then I would be held accountable if we failed to reach that goal. Not only did they tell me to resend the number, but they wanted me to apologize to the staff at our next meeting. I agreed to relay the message to my team but I changed my mind and told the truth of what the company thought. My team had my back so we decided to stick with the $1,000,000 projection. I also explained to my District Manager if we didn't hit $500,000 by mid-year, effective immediately, I would resign my position. He was very upset with me once I stated that but I knew my team and I had the ability to achieve our goal. By June of that same year, we had over $510,000 in sales and on track to hit $1 Million in sales for the year. We were on FIRE and rolling toward the $1 Million goal. We were only $100,000 away when upper management agreed to move the store from the left side of the street to the right side. It was a set up to ensure we would not meet the goal! They delayed putting up the new building signs as well as delayed the new merchandise. Even though I specifically asked them when I agreed to go to the store for an increase in merchandise, they did not do what I asked them to do. There were so many other things that were not done and it looked like we didn't have a chance to reach the goal for the year. Moving day took place the first week in January of the new year, and we were only $100,000 away from hitting our numbers for the entire year which would hinder my sales prediction from coming true. That means we needed to do $25,000 each week to do the million. So we are all moved into the new location directly across the street from the old building with no publicity, and we didn't even have a sign on the building. The first week we did $10,000, and things looked very bleak when it came to hitting the million dollar goal. The second week we did about $15,000, and then it dawned on me that I was being set up. Upper management was determined to see us fail. I decided to pick up the phone and call the President. I told him straight up that they were setting me up, but **nothing** was going to keep us from achieving the goal. Later that day both signs went up advertising the new location. Immediately, things took off, and we were back on track to hit the million dollar goal.

Our store was BUZZING! Customers from my old store that was only 12 miles away from the new store would come down and buy from us. I was intentional about building relationships with the local oil and gas businessmen. The relationships I built with my customer base was solid and I had nothing but faith in myself as well as my team. My team was so charged and on fire! I was loud and GUNG HO about the goal we were on track to hit regardless of the adversity. I would dance on tables like MJ and make the atmosphere fun for my team and enjoyable for the customers! So now it's the last weekend of the month and we needed $20,000 to hit the goal. On Friday we chopped it down to $10,000 going into Saturday but we still needed the rest before the store closed at 6pm. When the store closed, we were still $7000.00 away so I picked up the phone and called one of my longtime clients. He was a multi-millionaire and had spent thousands with me over the years. I told him that we needed $7000.00 to hit the number. He told me to pick out as much merchandise as needed to equal the $7000.00 and he would come over and pay for it in cash. And that's exactly what he did. We went approximately $100.00 OVER the $1,000,000 goal! When my client left the store we all went nuts! Yelling, laughing, hugging, cheering and celebrating! Our hard work truly paid off. We believed what we set out to do and we not only achieved our goal but exceeded the goal! It was a great year! I went on to win store manager of The Year which was the third most amazing accomplishment of my career.

The mistreatment wouldn't stop. About three months later, after achieving such a tremendous goal in the face of adversity, upper management put the first manager who I pleaded with for my job, back in power over me as District Manager. Really? He said I was incompetent and I knew he was going to be out to get me. This time, they scrutinized everything I did for the entire year even though I had achieved so much. Even the following year, my success was still prevalent and superior to that of all my peers. One day, the Vice-President, the one who thought I was incompetent, had a boss who began verbally abusing me while I was on the phone with him. His initial feedback was that even though we had a great year last year, I put too much pressure on my people and that I was too intense. The most ridiculous thing he said to me was, "You don't fit into *our* system." He also told me that it was a mistake that they gave me *store manager of The Year* but I could keep the trophy. I told him I was going to send the trophy back in order for the right person to have them and I was going to call the President to tell him the same thing. No matter what I said, he became even more belligerent and disrespectful to the point where I told him that I would not continue the call. After I hung up with him, I placed a call to the President. I told him, "The

Vice-President informed me you all made a mistake in making me *store manager of The Year*. I wouldn't want the person worthy of the award not have it, so I will wrap it up and ship it back to you. I will endure the abuse I am subject to but the numbers don't lie and I am as just as good as anybody and my work ethic has proven that over the years." So many lies had been told about me but I was determined not to give up. I remember sharing with my District Manager at the time, "You have systematically destroyed the careers of so many people who did not have the tenacity to endure your belligerent behavior. You have tried to assassinate my career and get me out of the company but I vow that there is nothing you can do to me to make me leave this company. I am going to be the only guy, the one person, no matter what you do to me, I am here for the long haul." I was determined to change the culture of the company. I refused to let them break me or destroy my career. My mind was fortified and my spirit strong. I was determined to maximize this opportunity no matter what. My brothers taught me the Teflon mentality so I was MADE for this. Suddenly, a miraculous intervention occurred. It was *the* most pivotal moment in my career other than being in total control and running my own store. I had several assistant managers who worked at my store but there was one gentleman, Big O, who was talented and full of wisdom. They took Big O out of my store to run another store in the absence of a manager being on vacation. Out of loyalty to me, Big O revealed that upper management approached him about my performance as store manager. He informed me I was being scrutinized and they wanted him to support the cause to bring me down. They were plotting to fire me but they needed him to agree to the false accusations that I was too overbearing and hard on my team. These accusations were not true and the way another person was being used to take down another person was insane. I was promoting and developing more people in an exciting and upbeat environment than any of my peers had ever done in the history of the company. I had no HR complaints from not ONE employee nor from my senior leaders at any point in time during my career. They went on to advise Big O he would get my store plus a significant pay raise if he would lie and say the things they were accusing me of were true. Big O told them, "No, I'm not gonna do that. If you are going to fire him, you're going to have to fire me as well because he's a great person and leader. He does a great job and everybody supports him 110%." They were totally outdone with the fact that he supported me so the meeting was immediately adjourned. Eventually, the members of upper management responsible for attempting to sabotage my career were demoted because of some of the poor decisions they were caught making. The District Manager (my first store manager) was caught taking the employees' money when gambling at his house. See how God works? He still had a plan for me even though their plan was to destroy me. God had another plan. I dedicate this portion of the book to "Big O" because if it wasn't for him, my career longevity would not be possible due to him not supporting the false allegations against me. Thank you from the bottom of my heart, "Big O".

There was another time when I was asked to move from my store AGAIN. The company decided to open an outlet store in the middle of Houston. I knew nothing about this new store being opened. At this point, my team and I were number one in the city at my current store. Things were going well, and my team was still on fire. So, my Regional manager said, "I need you to do me a favor. Before I go to my new position, I need you to go to another store in Midtown." I immediately said, "Absolutely not. I am not moving again after all of the things I've been through. We are number one in the city. Why would I go to another store that finished last place?" He proceeded to tell me that if I did not move, I was going to be fired. So my choice was to either move or lose my job. So, I went home that night feeling defeated. I told Diana, my girlfriend at the time, "I think they got the best of me. I'm gonna just quit." She told me, "No! Don't do that. You have proved them wrong so many times before now go to that other store and do it again." So I reluctantly accepted the position. The Midtown Store was off of Gessner in the middle of a run-down strip center next to a dry cleaners. I knew I had to find a way to win and build the right team.

One day, I ran across a young guy who had to be around 16 years old driving around trying to sell a stolen television. I said, "Hey, you need to get out of that lifestyle of crime. Go get rid of that TV and come back and get a job!" He told me, "I might steal from you." I told him, "You won't steal from me. People don't steal from people they like! You're hired!" He turned into a rock star! Eventually, he worked his way up to being one of the top store managers in the company at the age of 19. His wife went from being a sales associate to owning her own dentistry. Never underestimate the people you meet in the street.

So here I am again, starting from the bottom, working my way up. Upper management decided to open an outlet store in the midtown area and customers from all over the city flocked to it. Customers had the opportunity to come to my store and purchase top quality merchandise at discount prices. They were coming to this store from all around the city because they were disappointed by the selection at the outlet had a better selection but it didn't so outlet employees were sending customers to our store right down the street. Ha! Our store sales went through the ROOF! The Midtown location was the ONLY one that achieved its goal that year while every other store tanked! See how God works? They tried to do me wrong again and transfer me to another poor performing store, but God had a better plan!

From the very beginning, passion for the company and desire for accomplishments was at an all-time high. I started looking for the invisible possibilities that would help me grow my career. I noticed that there were major opportunities within the organization, one of them was the company didn't sell shoes at that time. I also knew that the number one customer service complaint in the fashion industry was the bottom of the slack. **One of the ways to sustain success is to solve a company problem**, so I created a plan to accommodate a variety of sizes with different foot patterns on a sheet of wood. I installed two heels so the customer could stand on top of the heel on the platform and have their slack properly measured. This invention revolutionized the customer service problems that the company was having. Once named, "The Harvey Heel Lift" and approved by the owner at the time, the invention went into mass production in order to stock each store with the new slack measuring system. I am humbled that I was instrumental in starting off selling shoes and because of our success, we began selling shoes in every single store across the country. There were many other revolutionary ideas that occurred in my career. From creating custom telephone greetings as well as changing operational procedures that made the organization millions and millions of dollars within a three year period. God used me to change operations that skyrocketed profits for the entire company. For example, my team and I had a vendor booth at a huge industry show where we were selling an item for well over the normal price. I took it upon myself to lower the price without the authorization of upper management. We ended up selling more of the item in two days than we had done in an entire year. I took a big risk making the executive decision to lower the price on every item, but because of my ability to be fearless, that one action changed the entire industry globally. To this day, we went from making $0.00 on this product after carrying it for a full year to turning that single product into a $700+ million business. I am so thankful to God for not allowing the organization to fire me and for giving me an opportunity to use their platform to create culture-shifting ideas. I have been blessed to receive countless team awards as well as individual awards over the span of my career. While there were good times, I had to endure being belittled and told on numerous occasions that I simply wasn't intelligent enough. I was told that I had to have a degree and a variety of other skill sets to qualify and excel in management in this business. I would like to share with you that I don't have a college degree. I think it's really good to require a degree to become a member of management, but there is also a better way to get to the top than just having a degree. I know a lot of intelligent people, even in this business, but you must have a really good understanding of the people, the process, and the profit. You must understand how the business is run to be able to prove to others that you are certified for the next level. Some people specialize in trying to keep you from fulfilling your purpose and destiny. Listen to me: do not allow these people to have power over you. Throughout this book, I have shared several times that when we believe the words of other people who put us down, we give them too much power by allowing them to affect us in a negative way. In actuality, their negative words are just the fuel you need to rise up to your greatness. I heard the negativity from my childhood and throughout young adulthood as well as when I became a full grown man. When we allow the negative affirmations of inability to accomplish the tasks to affect us, we fulfill the perceptions of what someone else thinks of our future. Do not allow anyone to rob you of your success. Take the negative words that they meant for evil and watch God turn things around for your good!

No Degree, But Still God Qualified

At this point, I thought I was going to get promoted to District Manager since I had been store manager. I had successfully exceeded every goal since starting with the company other than at the beginning of my career. So one day, we are at the first quarter meeting of the new year where upper management was going to announce the new District Manager. I was so sure I was going to be promoted, I even bought a new suit. Look at all of the invisible possibilities that I turned into millions of dollars in revenue for the company? From the Harvey Heel Lift to transforming how we answered the phones at the store to being moved from one low performing store to another, I knew I was qualified for the next level. So at the meeting, the Vice President of the company says, "Let me introduce you to your new District Manager…" Before he could finish, I stood up thinking he was going to call my name, but instead, he said, "Give it up for Ross Rail, everybody!" I quietly dipped down and sat back down in my seat. I was shocked!

Throughout my career, I have been faced with so many challenges and adversity. My supervisor underestimated my skill set and said very derogatory comments towards me regarding my inability to be a leader. There was one particular person with very obnoxious behavior who happened to be the Vice President for one of the companies I worked for. Never in a million years did I imagine that someone on his level would tell me to my face that I was uneducated and stupid. He was adamant about letting me know that I would not excel in this organization and that I needed to leave and move on. These derogatory comments took me off guard to a degree based on all the amazing things happening in my career. He had no idea that he was actually helping me succeed in spite of the negativity. He didn't realize that I was the type of person who was stimulated by the negativity which inspired me to fight everything he said. But he wouldn't target just me, he would take it upon himself to destroy so many other people with this type of approach. He used words in a vicious manner to destroy people's goals, dreams and other's drive to achieve greatness. I am mentioning this person, not to celebrate the negativity but to highlight that we must be careful how we treat other people. The universe has a way of coming back to rectify a person's life. It's sad that this person is no longer with us. Most people don't realize that when you do ugly things to other people, your life will never be all it needs to be. What goes around truly does come around.

So many of my supervisors refused to give me the opportunity to be promoted, but many were kind enough to tell me the things that I needed to know. I challenged many of them to tell me what I needed to know to qualify for different positions that I applied for. I was determined to show them that even though I didn't have a degree, I actually had the work ethic needed to master any job and achieve amazing results no matter the sacrifice. My superiors did not know that I had that strong work ethic embodied within me. Here's my philosophy regarding education and excelling in your career. The difference in obtaining an education is most people are disqualified from obtaining certain jobs because they don't have a college education, but my theory is if an individual takes the time to learn how a company is run and an opportunity presents itself for you to be promoted, you won't have to be discouraged from applying for the position. If you know how the company runs and understand operational manuals as well as the company culture, then you are more than qualified than the person who actually has a degree from a University. I am not knocking anyone with a degree but for those of you who may not want to obtain a degree, always remember that a person with a degree is not better than you. Many people disagree with that theory, but I am a witness that even if you don't have a degree, God has already qualified you, it's your birthright, just like he qualified me!

As humans, we often make excuses for not going to the next level by blaming society for our inability to succeed. We justify making poor choices just because we are a certain color. For a short period of time, I used to think the world was black and white based on how it was described and projected to me but I quickly learned that it's not. Just because I am a black man does not give me an excuse not to strive for excellence in everything I do. It is up to me to create a narrative for myself that guarantees that I significantly increase in value. I know that I have the power and mental fortitude, with my God and Savior's help in everything I do. No one can hold you back but yourself. Don't allow anyone to kill the dreams you have for your family, friends, or co-workers. You can do whatever you want to do in life to become the true you that you were made to be. Everyone has a purpose, including you.

Fearless goal-setting proves to the God of the universe that you are eligible to receive every good gift which comes from above.

6

Don't Get Ahead of the Universe

IF YOU DISCIPLINE yourself to have no expectations, then disappointment will never show up. Don't get ahead of the universe! Allow the universe to form itself and then align yourself with it. Rest assured, the universe will always ensure things will turn out the way they should as long as you are in rhythm with it. How much positive energy have you put into the universe? Except every outcome originating from situations that happen in life because that particular outcome is not always the end but rather the beautiful beginning of a process guiding you to reach your destination in life. It's imperative that you become fearless and confident as you set goals for your life so you can attract the best outcomes. A popular acronym for **FEAR** is *False Evidence Appearing Real,* and to crush fear, you must remove it as a barrier in your lives. Fearless goal-setting proves to the God of the universe that you are eligible to receive every good gift which comes from above. On the other side of fear is our true purpose in life!

I recall a time when I was just starting out in my retail career. I began setting goals that were critical to my success. I became obsessed with setting the proper expectations for my career moves and always remained clear of the path I desired to take. One day, I went to an engraving store and had my name engraved on a desk name plaque and right under my name I had them engrave the letters, "VP" right under it. I made a promise to myself that I would declare every morning that I would become Vice-President of the company. I paid attention to fashion trends and became extremely observant. Due to my fearless faith in the God of the universe, I ended up becoming the vice-president of three different companies simultaneously and founder of our own charity PEP Houston. I became Vice-President the same year and day Barack Obama became the First Black President of the United States...and he's left-handed just like me...WOW! This type of laser focus and commitment to God as well as holding myself accountable, has afforded me the opportunity to have amazing support at my company. I cannot take the credit for what I have been blessed to achieve. I am blessed to lead so many extraordinary people and have the honor of spending time with them along with their families. I made it my business to pay attention to everything happening all around me. My secret sauce was being relentless in my affirmations, impeccable with my word among my coworkers and completely aligning myself with the God of the universe.

Over the years, I have mentored hundreds of people, and many of them have similar goals they desire to accomplish.

What are some of the desires that most people put in the hat of the universe? They desire to:

- no longer be afraid of anything
- obtain their dream home (s)
- obtain their dream car (s)
- have more money
- have a long-lasting, healthy relationship
- have kids
- own a business
- become a pro-athlete
- be healthy
- attend or finish college

- become an actor or actress
- travel the world
- become a singer, rapper or movie star
- careers
- communicate better
- receive respect
- have a better relationship with God
- be a great sibling or family member
- be a great spouse or life partner
- write a book - (I did it! Yes! My first book that you are reading right now!)
- read at least one book per month
- overcome illness
- be happy
- LIVE LIFE

Do you see something you desire on this list? Take a moment to circle one or more of those items. Ok, now, repeat after me, **"I can do this, and I will NOT STOP until it's done!"** Didn't that feel good? You have to be sick and tired of being mediocre in order to achieve your goals in life. I know now that I was designed to be successful. I had never seen anyone close to me change their lives for the better. Successful people do the things unsuccessful people don't like to do. I realized that I was the one holding myself back. I was just afraid to make the change. Do you desire to achieve a better life faster? Put aside jealousy and build relationships with people who are doing better than you. Find out what they know and then do it!

I am honored to be able to share my story with you. My life has not been perfect by ANY means. I have made countless mistakes in my life along with my family members. My brother, Curtis, was in and out of jail multiple times and addicted to drugs after returning from the US Army. My brother, Kennith, joined the military after high school and even became Staff Sergeant as his career progressed. Unfortunately, he was honorably discharged due to a serious brain injury. My brother,

Keith also had a very successful military and business career. My brother, Julius was also in the US Army after a serious military accident and explosion that impacted him negatively. After being medically discharged from the U.S. Army, he became addicted to drugs and later on had a massive heart attack and triple bypass surgery. My sister, Sherry is a single-parent and the glue that keeps this family together. She is truly an amazing woman. I am not sharing this information to throw my siblings, my parents or anyone else under the bus because I love and respect everyone but I want you to have a clear picture that life has so many different turns and twists that you have the ability to overcome if you allow yourself to become aligned with the universe. It is very difficult and excruciating to live this life if you're not in tune with the universe. The universe reacts in response to the positive energy that radiates from the human experience. If you understand how the universe works and align yourself with it, you and the world become one. We all have our own destiny to fulfill, and some of us are truly living a blessed life because that's how it played out. On the contrary, in most cases, we are where we are due to the fact of us not really having the grace of God embedded in our hearts and following His lead. Many of us have been through certain obstacles that helped lead us to a consistent place of happiness, harmony, help, friendship, leadership and all the things that God promises in abundance if we align ourselves with the Creator of the universe and His Son, Jesus Christ, who gives us life.

Being open to feedback is a gift many people often overlook.

7

Be Open to Feedback

BEING OPEN TO feedback is a gift many people often overlook. I have learned to be open to feedback by giving other people permission to speak freely and state their point of view. Feedback is a gift because I am blessed with the opportunity to genuinely hear another person's perspective without judgment. You will be judged on how you judge yourself and others. I have always challenged people to be fair in order to receive respect from others. I have been blessed to mentor several individuals over the last three decades, and it is truly an honor to serve those who have the potential to go to the next level.

I am often asked to share my feedback or experience when mentoring others. I received an email from a colleague who said, "I'm mentoring a guy, who is in my opinion, a very together manager and someone with great potential. I would like to send him a list of a few things a manager can do to make it to the next level. I could create the list, but I would like yours if at all possible. After all, you have mentored me over the years and have made it yourself. I may be reaching out to other successful people as well. You're the first." I took a moment to process this question and I realize that in order to be successful there are some things that are absolutely non-negotiable:

1. You must possess a high level of integrity people can see. This is called CHARACTER.
2. Read every book you can about personal development but don't just read the information and never use it.
3. Listen without having a personal reaction. This is a major... shut up moment! You can't learn running your mouth or waiting to respond. This is why so many people have problems communicating with other people because they don't listen. There is nothing worse than a person pushing their opinion on you.
4. Be a spirited leader at all times. Don't wait until you are sick or about to die.
5. Transfer leadership as soon as possible to others. Succession planning is so powerful and if you don't realize it now, you will eventually. Do it now, before it's too late.
6. Dress the part at all times, everywhere you go.
7. Your friends and family are a reflection of who you will become. Don't do what you have seen others do. Create your own path and break the curse!
8. Be a giver. All the extra clothes in your closet and dresser drawers you haven't worn in ten years as well as food in the pantry please give it away this week. **Please do this now!**
9. Sacrifice yourself for other people first. Selfish people never accomplish anything long-term, and they are often lonely and unhappy
10. Take care of yourself and stay connected to your spiritual belief system. Take the time to meditate on God!
11. The two greatest powers on earth are ideas and air. How can this be? Let me tell you. Every single thing on earth is an idea including you and the earth. Think of something that has not been created. All you have to do is come up with the next big thing that people are interested in like the Apple iPhone. The next big idea you come up with can change the world. The best ideas we all see every day have been created like the

telephone pole, the airplane, and the light bulb. Even air is an idea that came from the Creator, and without it, nothing would exist on the planet…nothing! When air is properly used, it can be used to articulate a motivational speech that will move millions of people just like Dr. King's, "I Have A Dream" speech. What about individuals like Michael Jackson, Celine Dion and Whitney Houston who used their voices in the vehicle of air to transform the world? Some individuals use air to create wars and even domestic violence. When two people are yelling at each other spewing negativity, someone is bound to be hurt. Ideas and air are the two greatest powers on earth. There is a third power which is called, Free Will, but we will discuss that in my next book.

12. Value conversations by recapping what was discussed. Everyone who is a part of the conversation knows you value them as well as the conversation when you take the time to recap.

13. Always be open to feedback. This way you will always continue to get better. People see the real you but may not say anything, but they know the real you. If you are married or have girlfriends or boyfriends, and they have their act together take a moment just to shut up and listen. Being open to feedback shows humility.

This is not an all-inclusive list, but I believe these keys to success are most important when you are passionate about your next level in life, business, and relationships. The best way to identify unproductive behavior is to always ask for feedback. Talk to people you respect and admire and who knows you well. Ask them what they observe about your bad habits. Look for consistency. If you talk to ten people and eight of them say you never return phone calls on time, PAY ATTENTION! Your outward behaviors tell the real truth about you and if you are truly open to feedback. As we move forward in this chapter, take a journey with me as I share some more of my personal success stories along with the tools I've learned over the years and how I used feedback as a tool to go to the next level in my life.

The PEP Rally

The gift of motivational speaking has always been within me. I am so thankful that God has given me the opportunity to share my thoughts with the world through a program called, *People Enhancement Program* or PEP. PEP is a personal motto of mine where our philosophy is EVERYONE should be the CEO of their own lives and with that, enhancing the lives of those we are called to serve should be our number one priority. PEP came about based on my ability to galvanize and rally people of all races, ages, and socioeconomic status. Even in my professional career, I've used this same method to engage with my management team using the PEP model. Since I was an individual who struggled academically and didn't always perform at a high-level, I took it upon myself to ask my management for a promotion instead of waiting for them to offer it to me. I became the CEO of my own personal brand and wouldn't take, "NO" for an answer. They would say to me that I didn't have the skill set, the knowledge or the background to accomplish my goal of being promoted. For instance, I kept inquiring for years about becoming a multi-unit manager with one of the companies I worked for. I sent an infinite amount of emails (before that, I wrote handwritten letters) to upper management. I cannot tell you how many rejection letters I received saying things like, "At this time there are no positions available for which you are qualified for." Upper management told me to STOP sending letters because the President was tired of receiving them. I wasn't asking for a position I wasn't qualified for. All I was asking for was for them to give me an opportunity and if I failed, then I could understand. How could I increase my capacity to excel if I am never given an opportunity? No matter how many rejection letters I received, I continued to hold on to my faith in God as I pursued my goals. So I kept sending multiple letters until finally I was given the opportunity to interview for a District Manager position. They really didn't want me to have the job, but they promoted me anyway because they didn't have a choice. I was more than qualified for the job. All I wanted was an opportunity. I noticed the first sign of unfairness in the workplace when I was promoted. They gave me a $25 increase knowing at that time that amount was totally unfair for a District Manager with the level of responsibility I was going to be taking on. I knew there were other district managers making nearly double what they offered me, but I didn't challenge that because I wanted the privilege of having the position. Obtaining the position meant more to me than the financial gain. At first, I sat there for a second but then I said with the greatest enthusiasm I could muster up, "Gentlemen, I am privileged to take on the responsibility!" "Are you serious? You will take it?" they replied in disbelief. I replied, "That's a YES. The vision for this job has been made clear and I also know that you don't believe I can actually achieve this challenge. I just want to share with you that I'm not in it for the money, I'm in it for the opportunity to lead a group of men and women to do extraordinary things. I look at this amazing opportunity like a loaded gun with only one bullet. It's very clear that I only have one shot to be great and because your expectation is so low of me anything I do will be exceptional. But just know this, eventually, you will pay me what you owe me." So I took on the District Manager position and redefined the district's performance. Against all odds, we made it to the number one district in the company in less than six months. Then and only then, were they more than glad to give me an additional store. The only reason why they didn't give me a store, in the beginning, as they believed that I wasn't educated enough and that the store was already cultivated They did not believe that I could go to a store in East Texas and manage that store because it was a "cultural thing". They thought that if I took over the store, there would be a negative impact. Lo and behold, they gave me the opportunity! The store was added to the district and it became the highest performing district for that year transforming the entire market. Even though I continued to experience similar challenges throughout my career even to this day, I was determined to WIN and seize every opportunity as if it were my last chance! I used a concept called, "The Circle of Life" in my PEP Program which consists of establishing Spirituality, Family, Work, Personal Time and then right back to Spirituality. No matter what Higher Power you serve, you must establish spirituality above all things. I knew I could not achieve any level of sustainable success on my own so that is why I implemented the PEP Program and mastered the art of becoming the CEO of my own life to impact the lives of others!

24 Things I Live By Every Day

In order to become wildly successful, I believe every person must embrace becoming the CEO of their own lives and master the following characteristics:

1. **God:** God over everything! Love and respect God above everything.
2. **Care and Respect for Family:** Be the alpha male with my family by being a great provider and the best husband to my wife, Mattie.
3. **Optimism:** Once you discover your purpose you must maintain a positive attitude.
4. **Energy**: When you love what you do, you will have lots of energy to put into it, and you can work nearly non-stop!
5. **Warmth:** You must realize that everyone is important.
6. **Integrity**: You must be true to yourself and conduct all of your affairs with integrity.
7. **Trustworthiness:** Integrity leads others to you. You must earn trust by being worthy of it.
8. **Responsibility**: True leaders do not stop until the job is finished. They never make excuses. They may give reasons but not excuses.
9. **Self-Worth**: Leaders do not need outside confirmation of their worth. They know who they are and what they have to do.

10. **Knowledge:** Leaders have an insatiable appetite for knowledge which constantly expands the mind. A leader is a reader and leaders pursue wisdom.
11. **Submission:** When necessary, leaders must be followers, too.
12. **Self-Discipline**: Discipline involves meeting standards for a greater purpose. Self-discipline calls for self-imposed standards of excellence for a greater purpose. It calls for behavior change, denying yourself certain things to achieve something else.
13. **Morality:** A leader cannot be effective if they have moral failings. It zaps energy and destroys purpose. A leader does not have time to let personal or marital problems detract from the mission. Keep your house in order.
14. **Humor:** To be an effective leader, you have to laugh at life and not take it too seriously. Humor helps to win people over to your point of view. Smile at yourself and have fun. Be able to laugh at your mistakes and at things that you cannot control even in the midst of crisis.
15. **Resilience**: A leader has to be able to bounce back from a fall or catastrophe. Deal with it and get back in there.
16. **Experience:** A leader has a track record of success. Great leadership is defined by the results once they are given a task/ A Leader comes with a history. The problems you are going through right now are qualifying you for greater levels of leadership.
17. **Creativity**: Leaders know more than one way to solve a problem. Leaders are always suspicious of those who say, "This is the way" or "We've never done it that way or "It has to be done my way." A leader has the ability to walk around a learning opportunity and see it from 20 different angles. A leader loves new approaches, suggestions, and ideas even when they are not his/her own.
18. **Flexibility:** Leaders are not afraid to change. They know how to adapt and can make adjustments for other people's opinions,

needs, or comfort. Adjusting to others or to a situation is not a weakness but the epitome of strength.

19. **Humility**: A true leader does not care who receives the credit. Leaders are more concerned about results than awards, recognition, praise, or thanks for what they do.

20. **Courage:** A leader must be willing to take risks, to act on instinct, and to act alone when no one else will help. The leader also must be willing to do the right thing when no one else does it and make the call when no else will make a decision.

21. **Concepts**: Leaders see the big picture and do not let details overwhelm them. Leaders have a sense of being able to see concepts that no one else can see. They have the ability to see the invisible possibilities.

22. **Self-Image:** Dress the part at all times...no "Joe Bag of Donuts" image. They set the standard and take pride in doing it. For example, if you are a shoe consultant, always remember the customer is looking at yours first.

23. **Competitive:** Real leaders love and embrace competition-BRING IT ON!

24. **Caring:** Real leader, love and care for people and see no color.

You'll Know It When You Feel It

There is one characteristic I would like to highlight that is often taken for granted. It's that one thing that is common to every individual, relationship, team, family, organization, nation, economy, and civilization throughout the world. This one thing which, if removed, will destroy the most powerful business, the most thriving economy, the most influential leadership, the greatest friendship, the strongest character and the deepest love. On the other hand, if developed and leveraged, that one thing has the potential to create unparalleled success and prosperity in every dimension of life. Yet it is the least understood, most neglected and most underestimated. That one thing is TRUST. So what is trust? You know it when you feel it. Former CEO of Mattel, Robert Eckert said, "As you go to work, it is your responsibility to build trust." We have the tendency to judge ourselves by our intentions and others by their behavior. Typically, behavior is the manifestation of motive and agenda. The behavior that best creates credibility and inspires trust is acting in the best interest of others. When we do so, we clearly demonstrate the intent of caring and the agenda of seeking mutual benefit. And this is where the rubber meets the road. It's easy to say, "I care" and "I want you to win" but it is our actual behavior that demonstrates whether or not we mean it. It's difficult to trust others if you aren't trustworthy. The more trustworthy you become the more you will attract those who can be trusted.

Run!

In life, we encounter people who should be avoided. These individuals are toxic to your success. Not only should you run from them but be sure not to become one of them. **RUN** from these type of people:

1. People who other people do not respect. Run!!
2. People who don't listen. Run!!
3. People who always have something negative to say. RUN faster, please!!
4. People who speak positively about you in front of you and discredit you behind your back. Run!!
5. A person who always asks for you to do something but never wants to help...they'd rather complain. Run! Run!
6. A person who can't admit to his or her mistakes but make you feel bad when you make a mistake. RUN!!! Can someone open the door for me?!
7. A person who likes borrowing money and never pays you back. Run!!
8. A person who never has gas money or can't pay the rent or stick you with the check on a dinner or lunch outing. (I just tripped running away from you!)

Gravitate!

There are certain people you should gravitate to:

1. People who are committed to empowering others to make extraordinary things happen
2. People who are always engaged in personal development
3. People who always have positive energy
4. People who always follow up and keep their promises
5. People who have positive people around them.
6. People who take care of other people during a crisis.
7. People who have strong spiritual beliefs.
8. People who you know are better than you.
9. People who read books.
10. People who make great investments.
11. People who eat right and exercise.
12. People who work with charities.
13. People who pray and meditate.
14. People who are entrepreneurs.
15. People who travel the world.
16. People who love reading the Bible.
17. People who love Jesus Christ and God The Father.

There is so much controversy going on in the world right now, and there are very few people who agree to focus on the good and embrace the daily responsibility of uplifting others.

8

Just Thinking

HAVE YOU EVER been driving along in your car and had a "just thinking" moment? Perhaps you were thinking of a meeting you had to prepare for once you arrived at the office or as you were driving home from work you were thinking about what to have for dinner. What about those times when you were thinking about your problems and how you were going to resolve them? But what happens when those ordinary thoughts are interrupted by profound, extraordinary thoughts that burst into your mind? Those "aha" moments that make you say, **"WOW...that's powerful! I have to share this with the world!"**

My "Just Thinking" motto became a way of life for me to evolve as a man and carry-on successfully during my life's journey. These "mindful moments" are thoughts that simply come to me and motivates me to be successful. I am excited to share with you how to take those "ordinary" thoughts and make them extraordinary in your everyday life. "Just thinking" evolved as a vehicle for me to send out positive notes to other people keeping them focused on the good in life. There is so much controversy going on in the world right now, and there are very few people who agree to focus on the good and embrace the daily responsibility of uplifting others. These notes acted as positive stimulators in the workplace and in everyday life. I became even more passionate about communicating high levels of positivity to everyone in my sphere of influence so that they would have some form of consistent, supportive, and encouraging thoughts that would develop their minds to be inspired every day. These notes also challenged me to think of original thoughts that would be activated by situations and circumstances that I may experience throughout the course of the day. I was determined to change the culture because there was nothing I could do about the past but I could sure influence the future.

Just Thinking...Situations vs. Problems

One day I was reflecting on my 50 plus years of life and I remembered the first "Just Thinking" note I ever wrote. It was called, *"The Learning Opportunity"*. I discussed the benefits of embracing the learning opportunity in Chapter 2 but I wanted you to see how your thinking patterns can grow into concepts that help shape your future and the destinies of those around you. I wrote that first note because I wanted to look at problems and change how people see them in their minds but I first had to change my own perspective about how I saw problems. I established the concept that everything happens for a reason and when people see things they consider to be problems, they will always be disappointed. The truth is, there really are no problems but instead they should be reframed as "situations" that are occurring in order for God to expose the extraordinary gift within you.

The earth's population spends too much time thinking negatively and reacting to situations with their feelings. Unfortunately, we live in a "feelings-based" society where you are taught to "do what you feel" but sometimes you have to take a moment to just think before you make a move. There are others who make more logical and rational decisions because they understand that "feeling-based" conversations and decisions will normally place you in a predicament that may be tough to get out of. Let me give you an example: when a person says, "I have a problem" that's a "feeling-based" statement but when a person says, "I have a learning opportunity" that person is saying they are open to sharing and receiving sound wisdom and fundamentals to resolve the situation at hand. The more you talk about the problem the more anxiety will take over the situation and your mental capacity to think creatively and find the learning opportunity will diminish greatly. Now, I am not encouraging you to walk around like a zombie without feelings, but I want you to be more concerned with doing the opposite of what you feel and execute the positive in that moment. Every opportunity you have to solve a "problem" is a gift. You have been given an inner ability to resolve every challenge that comes your way but you must be more practical AND positive in your thinking and LESS reactive in your approach to ALL situations. Remember, everything happens for a reason so if it is happening to you, there is a learning opportunity that you need to embrace. The universe is going to respond to the calculation that has already been established but your response can literally change the outcome of any situation. Let me paint a better picture for you: The universe, as well as the world, is a mathematical equation based on a numerical system so everything is systematically calculated and cannot be seen by the natural eye. Everything has its own DNA structure and calculation, even those opportunities you see as problems. Removing a portion of any mathematical equation will change the outcome of everything especially those things moving in rhythm with the universe. A temperamental attitude also calculates and most people would normally say things that change the calculation of the moment. So if you have a problem, the calculation for a positive outcome will change if you have a negative response, on the other hand, if you have a positive response, you will have a positive outcome. For example, if you are shooting hoops and notice that you just can't miss, your mind is in rhythm with the universe. Let's say you are playing golf or tennis and you notice you are consistently winning, you have found that zone. But then there are those other times when you're not in a zone and you find yourself ahead of the universe and everything freezes. You notice certain things not working in your favor especially for those who specialize in being temperamental and wearing their emotions on their sleeve.

Have you ever heard someone say, "Good people are hard to find"? Well, in theory, they are correct, but the reality is, "good people" don't want to work for the person who has that kind of negative thinking. The truth is, it is NOT hard to find good people because if you are somebody worth working with, good people would be flocking to work for you because of your positive perspective on life. Yes, it is hard to find good people if that's the way you think, but bad people will **never** find good people to do extraordinary things. Bad people are those who are constantly being negative in their speech and lack the faith to see and do the impossible. Bad people are unable to influence people to sacrifice 8, 10 or 12 hours of their lives on a daily basis in a career or a community initiative because of their "stinking thinking" and negative reactions to those situations they call "problems." The "just thinking" motto helps motivate others to look at the world in a way that it hasn't been looked at before because there is a battle in your brain where choosing positivity over negativity is happening every moment of your life. You must discipline your mind to avoid "stinking thinking" because it will take over and send you into a dark, deep path of confusion that can clog the brain from receiving the learning opportunity that is needed to take you to the next level in life. Just thinking positively will help bring creative logic to solve all "problems" with ease and grasp the learning opportunity from the very beginning.

Just Thinking...What Society Calls "The Education System"

Every time I drop my youngest daughter, Madison, off at school each morning, I encourage her to be the **best and not like the rest!** I want everyone that I know to be the best no matter what. I was just thinking about how society has a way of programming our children as they grow up to go to school, graduate from high school and college, graduate again and then secure a job. There are other people who teach their children to grow up and own a business. They refuse to program them to work for someone else. A small percentage of our society has created a false perception with our children after going to school for an extended period of time; they are then expected to find a job, but when they graduate from college, in many cases, there are no jobs in the field they have studied in. There are many cases where education didn't help you secure the job because many companies are looking for someone with additional experience. How would a person obtain additional experience if they are fresh out of college? Something is wrong with this picture, and we need to start educating our children to grow up and establish their own businesses. We must help our children find their passion and not be subject to a system that creates followers, not leaders.

We all are leaders but we just have to be able to tap into it. Leadership is an attitude and a way of life. I began realizing over a period of time that I couldn't remember any of my teachers from elementary, middle or high school except Reverend Dr. Leon Eichelberger. He was the only teacher that I could remember out of my entire educational career and I was just thinking about how he made such a dynamic impression on me. He never called me stupid or made me feel dumb if I did not perform like some of the other students. He allowed me to be myself and learn at my own pace. He taught me that I had choices in life and not to let the education system define me. There are many people who were not as fortunate as I was to have a Dr. E in their lives. He not only taught me how to be successful but he SHOWED me how to do it. He taught me not to embrace what others had to say about me but he wanted to know what I thought about me! Dr. E not only had a major impact on my life but he also impacted the lives of so many others. So many people have been so scarred by the education system based on the fact that after spending an hour with the teacher over the course of a school year, "educators" evaluate you and give you a grade that is often a misrepresentation of who you really are and not taking into account how you learn. How can someone grade you after only taking one test label you for the rest of your life? There are a lot of people who are destroyed because they do not have the academic validation of a passing grade. Many of these people have been labeled "stupid" and often scarred for life because of teachers who misinterpreted how they learned. While there are some awesome teachers in the world in spite of the flaws in our education system, there are some who refuse to show and explain to children ways to be successful in school and life like Dr. E did for me. If that child happens to obtain a "D" or maybe even an "F" on their record, not because they were in class goofing off but because they were misunderstood. Now your child is looked at as a "failure" or maybe even has a learning disability just because they learn differently from the other students. I find this ridiculous because some of the same English teachers can't maintain a healthy romantic relationship because they are unable to effectively communicate or they just simply lack personal interaction skills to impress other people. What about the math teacher who cannot balance his or her own checkbook? The math teacher who cannot make good financial investments because they are a complete mess. How can we allow these people to have the authority to inaccurately label an innocent child? The chemistry educator who has to hire a pool guy to properly balance the chemicals in their pool because they can't do it? Consider the health teacher who fails to take care of themselves by overeating? They are obese but they are given the authority to define our children's fate for the rest of their lives? There are so many other examples I could talk about concerning the education system but I think you get the picture. Then there is the student who may achieve an academic grade above the standard and those same "educators" see the A/B student better than the C, D or F student. I have met some of the most educated people who go into the real world and are often unequipped when they faced. Many of those same A/B students who felt the pressure to perform in the education system became addicted to drugs just to be able to maintain that feeling of achievement. Many of those considered academically superior to others often go into the real world with their double majors and graduate degrees totally unable to cope with the situations that being in a corporate environment brings. I'm puzzled by this because one would "just think" that a person who has successfully gone through the education system that they really would have their lives together. I have a difficult time understanding how an "educator" who teaches our children concepts on a daily basis do not apply those same concepts to their own lives. We cannot leave our identity up to someone else. "Stupid" is a label that someone gives another based on what "they" think is intelligence or success. My "just thinking" principle that I want our children to capture is this: your life will be 100 times better if you refuse to allow some other person to define you.

I have witnessed married couples going to counselors, who to them, they have been divorced multiple times looking for them to help save their marriage. How can a person who has poor relationship habits of their own help you heal in your marriage? My point is this, it's not enough to just know to do the right thing and "just think" about doing the right thing but we have the responsibility to practice what we preach. I want you to just think and always look for the invisible possibilities **inside of you** and understand who you really are. I want you to be convinced about the gift you are to the world. I don't care what kind of grades you received in school. It's all about how you impact this world and how to unleash the potential that's already inside of you. God is the manufacturer of our very being and HE has the true owner's manual which demonstrates how we operate within the earth. We often ask other people how to be effective or we want them to define who we are but you can't go to someone else and expect them to "fix" your problem when it's very clear that they are not the Creator. The Cadillac luxury car dealership is the only authorized dealer that can take care of a Cadillac. The average consumer has never read the entire owner's manual of their vehicle and never will look at it. But if you did, you could operate your vehicle more efficiently. Your vehicle would also last longer, if you took the time to read the manual. God made us the same way. He created the Bible as the operational manual for every human being. It has everything that we need to operate our lives. If we choose to embrace this manual, you will live a superior life experiencing joy, satisfaction and fearless living. I've discovered by just thinking, that everything we need to understand about who we *really* are is not found in a classroom but found in the chief manufacturer of all things who is God and the creator of the original Owner's Manual, The Bible. No single individual has the ability to help us perform at our highest possible level other than Jesus Christ. With The Maker's Mind, ALL things are possible if we would just believe. Walk by faith, not by sight.

Just Thinking...Profiling

I found myself in a variety of situations as I established my roots in Houston. I had been detained several times for no valid reason, and I have every right to tie it back to racial profiling or Driving While Black. I have experienced random checks in a variety of different scenarios and racial profiling on two occasions. Once for a false DWI in which I was found not guilty and the second occasion was when I was pulled over for a suspended driver's license from my Hometown. I had been living in Houston for almost 12 years at this point, and I had my Texas driver's license the entire time. My license had never been suspended nor had I allowed it to expire. One day, a police officer pulled me over and arrested me for a suspended driver's license. To this day, I do not know why he pulled me over because I was not speeding and I obeyed all traffic laws. I didn't even receive a ticket he just arrested me on the spot. When I asked the officer why he was taking me to jail, he told me because of my suspended driver's license. I asked the officer how I could be driving around for 12 years in Houston with a suspended license from my Hometown and apply for a license in the state of Texas? So he took me to jail, but I was later released on bail the same day. They gave me a court date scheduled for a few weeks later. I arrive to court, and explained to the judge that the police officer told me to keep my driver's license, so he knew then my license was not suspended. Even when I showed him and explained that my current license was not expired, he still took me to jail anyway. When you have a suspended license, your license is supposed to be taken by the police officer when you are arrested. The judge says to me, "Mr. Harvey, we owe you an apology. Apparently, there was "glitch" in the system. Your license was never suspended." The judge had no choice but to drop the charges!

I want to highlight two more pivotal points in my life that have to deal with certain perceptions and perspectives we often make excuses for. Did you know I came up against prejudice from a black person? When I was applying for a job with a retail company in the early '80s, this particular gentleman who was the Regional Manager at the time, said whenever he hired black people (as if he wasn't black) they would always screw him over or try to get his job. So he told me to get out of his office and obtain more experience in the field of retail. Which was shocking moving from Harrisburg, PA to the South because I was always told that people in the south were much nicer! How is it I needed to gain more experience when I already had three years of experience? So I left and went to work at a shoe store.

About four years later, I applied to the same company after an ad was posted in the newspaper for a Training Manager position. Once I arrived at their corporate office, I entered the building and sat in the very same lobby four years prior. The same man walked out of his office and said, "Don't I know you?" and I said, "Yes." He said, "From where?" I said, "I'm the gentleman you told to get out of your office and go get more experience!" So he told me to step into his office to ask me several questions. "So if I give you this job, you promise not to fuck me over or try to take my job like most black people try to do?" I said, "No, Sir. I don't have anything to do with anyone else trying to come in here and take your job." He wanted to be sure that if he gave me this opportunity, I needed to be committed to him and that I would not do that to him. I made it very clear to him that I was going to show him that I am not that person, **but I'll come back to that later on in the story in just a moment.**

Three years prior to when the guy told me to leave his office and get more experience, I applied to a shoe store in Sharpstown Mall. After applying, the District Manager called me and told me to meet him at the shoe store. Once I arrived, the store manager thought I was a manager from the corporate office, and I was shocked at how he treated me. He was with a customer but stopped interacting with the customer to invite me into the store. He escorted me to the back room and asked me to sit in his office. As I sat down, he picked my feet up and put them on the desk. He even gave me the morning paper. He told me to read the paper until the District Manager arrived. At this point, I wanted to share with him that I was someone else but he was moving so fast and never gave me an opportunity to explain myself. After a short while, the District Manager arrived and said, "Hey, I see you met your new potential help?" Once the store manager found out that I wasn't the new Corporate Manager, he lost his mind. During the interview, he just kept staring at me and was quite upset. Once the DM was done with the interview, he hired me for the salesperson position paying $5.00 and commission on accessories. The DM made his final points and said his goodbyes and exited the store. The store manager proceeded to call me a nigger as the DM was walking out the door. I was in total shock! This was a major defining point in my life to move south to be called a "nigger" for the very first time in my life. I wanted to retaliate, and I had so much inside of me that I wanted to say to him. I know that was a moment where I could have looked at the entire situation as a "problem," but instead, I looked at the entire situation as a learning opportunity. I told the store manager to his face that day, "_ANYBODY can be a nigger, including you._". I also told him that I wouldn't accept his "gift" of words nor the negative titles that people try to give me. I understood he had done this to people before me, but I made it clear to him that I don't believe anything that does not elevate me. I was determined to stay there and do an amazing job until I took his job. I let the District

Manager know the same thing over the phone that they can't do or say anything causing me to react or resign. I explained to him I would stay working for this company until I take the store manager job. I believe God came down and connected with me and caused me to respond in such a profound way. I simply responded by saying and made it VERY clear to him that, I became Assistant store manager six months after being hired. About a year and a half after that, I was managing the Westwood Mall shoe store when suddenly I received a call from the District Manager, asking me to come to Almeda Mall to meet him the following day. When I arrived at the store, I asked Rob, another salesperson, where the DM was. I was informed that he was in the shoe stockroom. As I entered the stockroom, the DM who hired me remembered I told him and the store manager I was going to stay with the company until I obtained the store manager job and that day had come. The DM told the auditor who was completing the audit of the stockroom, "Do you know Chaseray told me and the store manager that he was going to stay here until he took his job? At the time I didn't believe that, and now, two years later, he did it. He is now managing the biggest store in the city, and the other store manager has officially been fired. And I'm the one he told after telling the store manager he would do it."

Remember the gentleman who made me pledge my loyalty to him at the retail fashion store and promise not to take his job? Well, he became so threatened by my presence (I didn't know this at the time) until he ended up being removed. So many people are destroyed by the negative words and attitudes of parents, supervisors, and co-workers. I'm telling you, don't let it happen to you anymore! Why? Because this is the fire we all have to go through to be shaped into what we will become in life. So many people fail this major life test. I'm so glad I didn't. In no way am I telling you to accept the verbal abuse from negative people. Nothing good ever happens to a person with a negative mindset. Stop being negative to yourself and anyone else! I'm very passionate about you knowing how to respond and having confidence in very difficult situations. I also challenge you not to stay in the same position your entire career and not choose to be great at it! Trust God to make the way, because no one can do it on their own

I continued to accelerate my performance in my career all because I learned how to respond and not react when situations occurred. What I want you to know is this: it would have been so easy for me to retaliate and be justified in my actions just so I could feel better about what happened to me but that is not something I chose to do. I challenge you to take the defining moments when people say horrifying things to you and use that moment to MASTER adversity. Remember when I shared with you in Chapter 1 about my childhood and how I complimented my family members for calling me stupid? Listen, we can tie our emotions to anything to validate our feelings, but you must remember that everything is happening in this world for a reason, even racism. We make excuses for allowing racism and negativity to exist when in actuality if we'd take ownership and treat each other fairly we can ALL win. If each of us would take ownership to do the right thing toward one another, we will always outnumber the bad elements in this world if we would just come together! I wholeheartedly believe that if we STOP REACTING TO STUPIDITY and learn to respond with truth and love, we can change this world in one day. We can sit and complain about the craziness happening all around us, but there must be a collective gathering of the majority of good people who make things right. If we bind together, we can influence the people in power to make negativity, such as racism and negativity against the law. If we all take a moment to change negative perspectives about other races, our entire world will change in an instant!

Be careful not to let your brain subscribe to the dark side of problems that are presented to us in this world but see the blessing and learning opportunity in every situation. Sometimes we become frustrated when we actually need to take a step back and say, **"What am I supposed to learn at this moment?"** Refer back to the "Just Thinking" moments in this chapter when you feel like calling it quits.

Always remember that challenges are great opportunities to show you exactly what you are made of. Complaining all of the time will NEVER solve a problem nor will a learning opportunity present itself. Pay close attention to those who complain versus those who look for the opportunity to grow in challenging moments. ALWAYS continue to feed your mind with positive thoughts, and you will never lose it. Having great character is the key to succeeding. Here's how you find out if you have great character: if a person gives you access to power, money or sex, watch how you respond to these three elements over time. Most people change instantly! They are the worst ones who don't have great character. Good character was first given to us when God said, "Let's make man in the image of me." That is true character.

Just Thinking...Patience

Just remember, when you ask for more patience, more difficult things show up. Sometimes, you don't understand why you are going through challenging times, but that was the prayer request. When you pray for patience, always expect challenges.

Just Thinking...God's Help

When you ask God to help you, He dispatches other people to assist you. Most people never notice that's why we were created, to be dispatched to help others. We are not only dispatched to help others during difficult times, but we are also required to help them fulfill their true purpose in life.

Just Thinking...Personal Development

People with low self-esteem can come up with all sorts of excuses to avoid taking the first steps to a better future. Don't let this be you. Every day we should do our best to help people become better at what they do...that's Servant Leadership! We are all called to do better in life, and we do not have time to allow low self-esteem to rob us of our heart's desires. Think about it: do you have to go to school to become smarter or <u>secure a job to improve your lifestyle, family, yourself and much more...REALLY?????</u>

Just Thinking...Leadership

One day, I was asked by a colleague to share the "Do's and Don'ts" of building a great team. I truly believe the team leader needs to establish a common goal that everyone can participate in once it has been established. It is imperative that each member of your team has an opportunity to exercise their skill set and potential as the goal is being pursued. The next thing that needs to happen is to find and discover the fundamental principles that everybody can respect and live by daily. Principles that are good and sound will encourage the group to live up to their full potential. As the team leader, we have to exhibit and embody the philosophy that has been established in order to keep the rest of the team inspired, interested, involved, and committed to accomplish the common goal. The joy of victory will be experienced when our daily actions are consistent which will inspire the team members on a daily basis because we as leaders are exhibiting what we are communicating with the team.

Do's of Building A Great Team

1. Establish principles that are solid, clear and fair for everyone to see and feel.
2. Be encouraging, inspiring, and spontaneous with your positive feedback.
3. Highlight hidden potential and teach them not to believe anything that does not empower you.
4. Leaders need to be true examples- be the person everyone wants to be around.
5. Give consistent and authentic recognition.
6. Encourage your team to take good notes and pay attention to detail to create that WOW factor.
7. Have a positive attitude that is contagious and that creates motivation in others at all times.

8. Be a great listener. Write down their ideas, share them with the decision makers and give THEM credit!
9. Let others feel the JOY of winning without getting in the way.
10. Communicate in a way that inspires and unleashes the winner within.
11. Be fair and put your team first!
12. Be sincere and authentic when you apologize when you are wrong. Take ownership of the offense.

Don'ts of Building a Great Team

1. Don't be selfish. It's not about YOU...it's about the TEAM achieving the GOAL.
2. Be sure to always have a clear plan.
3. Don't avoid exhibiting the principles you talk about.
4. Don't be unappreciative.
5. Don't be emotional and reactive.
6. Don't complain all the time by telling other people what they need to do better.
7. Don't be guilty of not listening or take notes when being coached.
8. Don't refuse to follow direction.
9. Don't be a know-it-all.
10. Don't undermine others.
11. Don't refuse to apologize when you have offended someone.
12. Don't be guilty of creating lose-lose situations. Be a MASTER at win-win-win strategies.

If you are in management, activate these **3 Key Traits** with your subordinates:

1. Don't talk down to them.
2. If you want to be liked, be likable.
3. If you want to be respected, be respectable.

Leadership News You Can Use

- A great manager brings out the greatness in each of their subordinates. Your manager should be training you on something new every day!
- Defective leadership always attempts to use authority to control people. Don't allow anyone to exercise control over you and become the "Benefactor."
- Great management in action is the ability to promote others to the next level!
- When a person becomes a passionate visionary for the benefit of others, that person is an authentic leader!
- You know you're an effective leader when you are able to communicate a vision in such a way that your entire team takes ownership of it.
- High five someone at least ONCE per day!
- Send a thank you card once a month to the people that impact your life in positive ways.
- Each and every day, notice the good in people and then tell them you see it.
- Every member of a company should make taking care of people the number one priority and if you witness your leaders not doing it, call them on it in a professional manner.
- The key to being successful in management is treating people like ADULTS. Some managers treat employees like kids. When people are treated like people, they tend to behave in a professional manner.
- A true leader makes themselves increasingly unnecessary. True leadership is measured, not in your presence but in your absence.

My ultimate goal as a leader is not to perpetuate followers but to help create other leaders. A good leader reduces the follower's dependency on the company by always following up to see if they are doing their jobs right or not at all. Leaders should measure his or her success and effectiveness by the diminishing degree of his or her follower's dependency on him or her. The less the leader is needed, the more effective that leader truly is.

Just Thinking...Hiring and Promoting The Right People

The careful selection of the people on your staff is critical to your future success. Select the right people, and your job as a manager will become a lot less complicated. Your stress levels will noticeably diminish, and you'll have a lot more fun. If you select the wrong person, you will only compound your current problems. Of course, you must take into account other factors such as attitude, honesty, integrity, and previous track records. Be careful NOT to select someone just like you. Remember, you want this person to complement your skills. Hiring someone with the same likes and dislikes will most likely create a bigger mess. Controlling people usually have the wrong mindset. Typically, people who are controlling believe no one can do a thing better than them. Don't be the kind of person who refuses to delegate. With proper training and good communication on a daily and/or weekly basis, the well-chosen team will do the tasks you have asked of them and in many cases outperform YOU. Gleefully surrender to someone with better organizational ability and a passion for looking after the details of moving the team forward. My final point is; hire the right people, train them, hold them accountable and then learn to let stuff go. Learning to let stuff go is the Test of All Tests as it relates to your mental freedom.

Just Thinking...The Right Mindset

Changing your mindset is truly the foundation for incredible conversations that lead to exceptional success. Self-awareness is the first step to changing a negative mindset. You can achieve the greatest leaps in performance and take your results from average to extraordinary by changing your assumptions and perspectives and behaving accordingly. The ability to communicate with customers, employees, friends and even family requires systems and skills that are built on the right mindset. How is your mindset right now? Stop blaming everyone else. You are the only one who can make YOU great! Can we have a conversation without excuses? When you know someone is great, you can have a conversation about them without saying, "But." So I challenge you now to say all of the most positive things you can say about a person without saying "But" to give your personal recommendation or endorsement.

Just Thinking...Brain Logic

I am elated about helping people approach the world in a way that it hasn't been looked at before. Please understand that the battle going on in your mind right now is a constant thing for all of us. If you are not thinking of ways to bring logic to your mind every day, then it will take over and send you into a deep, dark place of confusion that controls you for a lifetime. This is why we are codependent to our families, jobs and so much more. We were born with zero limitations. Why? Because God made us that way. For example, you were born as a baby with zero limitations until you met your parents who started the limitations program on you. With all the "you can't do this" or "you can't do that", they inflict fear and intimidation on you brainwashing you from living up to your full potential. Here is where the life limitations end for everyone, including me. Regain control of your mind and stop letting people who came before you be a poor example of what you can or cannot do because it will destroy you. Join God and me in changing the world one person at a time. This is a major test we all have to go through to live on the other side. Take control today and stop letting self-doubt and other things control you. Life is going to end here on this planet for all of us one day. Your quality of life is based on how you communicate with yourself and what you focus on determines how you feel.

Just Thinking...LIFE

Remember, if you let negative things you see and hear control you, you will never understand how great you are already. Validation is not given to you. And if you believe it and desire it, you will lose everything including your mind. Let the Universe play out the way your life should be. That way you are always in sync so that it can lead you to your true destiny. When things happen to challenge you to become a better person, insecurities are minimized leading you to the path of success.

- Just think about how many times you have overreacted to find out later it didn't turn out the way you thought it would?
- Live and know you are one of the greatest human beings on planet earth. The fact is you are the world's greatest commodity.
- Don't allow your emotions to control you.
- Enjoy life, and it will enjoy you back! Do special things for yourself. Chances are, nobody else will be as special at how you treat yourself.
- If you spend more time working on your weaknesses, all you end up with is a lot of strong weaknesses. Celebrating your weaknesses does not give you a competitive edge in the marketplace. Focus on your brilliance and practice your skills until you reach your desired results.
- If you copy the technique of champions, you too can become a champion!
- Remember to really care about people every day! That's what will make you a special person in life!!!
- If you REALLY care about people, you will respect them.

Be aware of the habits that are not working for you! Some of the habits that may be holding you back could be:

- Stealing
- Eating at irregular times of the day
- Not taking enough time off for fun and family--guilt free
- Living life without hugging your spouse, children and/or pets
- Being mean and rude to others

- Hitting the snooze on the alarm several times in the morning
- Telling everyone you are not a morning person
- Going to work hungry
- Feeling swamped instead of asking for help
- Borrowing money from other people and never paying it back
- Talking instead of listening
- Not returning phone calls on time
- Being late for work and meetings
- Poor communication skills
- When asked a question, you do not respond truthfully
- A lack of clarity regarding goals and expected outcomes
- Not attending to paperwork quickly and efficiently
- Forgetting someone's name within sixty seconds or less after being introduced to them
- Allowing others to speak negatively about others to you
- Gossiping over the phone, social media and in person
- Controlling the SMALL stuff you need to let go of
- Overuse of your cell phone on social media
- Not dressing for the occasion every single day
- Always complaining
- Not following through on time with the things you promised to do
- Having to be told to do the same thing repeatedly but you never change
- Having a bad attitude
- Smoking and drinking so much to the point where you have zero energy to perform to the best of your ability

Just Thinking...Put Yourself First If No One Else Will

In order to be truly successful in life, you must take care of yourself with the proper diet and exercise. In what ways can you promote a better you? Of course, you could drink energy drinks and coffee six or seven times a day, but you are seriously putting your health at risk. Hypertension, obesity and other side effects may occur. You may feel great at the moment, but you can have a tough time relaxing and truly feeling your best self. Exercise is the best way to promote optimal health. 99% of successful people have a workout regimen. The fastest way for God to water the seed He has placed inside of you is to take care of the vessel it is housed in.

What are the benefits of exercising?
- Improves your sleeping habits
- Increases your energy levels
- Relieves stress and anxiety
- Protects against injury
- Promotes a healthy posture
- Relieves digestive disorders
- Enhances your self-image
- Expands your longevity

Just Thinking...Love Cannot Be Defined

My love for my wife cannot be defined. Most people believe that true love can be explained and defined. Once you try to define love you cancel it out because love is undefinable. There are two different perceptions of love: Some people are in love with the chemical adrenaline, not with the person. When the drug of adrenaline goes off in the body, you start thinking you are falling in love. When the adrenaline wears off, some people realize they were more attracted to the other person based on their physical make up. You're not in love if a person walks out of your life and you completely fall apart, becoming ineffective and despondent with yourself. That is not the way love should be. True love has no definition; it's something that can't be explained. You don't know love exists until it is tested. For example, if your spouse or partner asked you to do things that you normally wouldn't do and you feel joy in doing them, that's love. When you do anything they request without question, it is the closest thing to true love. When you go the extra mile and sacrifice your needs for the relationship, these are indicators, not a definition, of what true love is. When I fell in love with my wife, we decided to not have sex until we became husband and wife. We wanted to know for sure our undesirable need to be together was real. We took the time to really enjoy each other's company by eating off the same plate, laughing together, enjoying similar interests like ice cream and activities in fashion. We both share an overachiever mindset and desire to put forth hours of work to accomplish our common goals. We work hard to put our family first as well as celebrate each other first. We have become one and we choose not to be separated at any point. Love is not a feeling, it's what you do. When you're truly in love, you love YOU first! Love yourself so much that you can share your love with someone else.

I discovered true happiness when I submitted to myself more so I knew how to love my wife and others. We cherish every moment we have together by being intentional in everything we do. At the center of our marriage and family is the art of goal setting. Every year, we sit down and write everything we plan to accomplish for the next year. We decided to be intentional in developing our family and strengthening our relationships, so we set goals each year. Once the goals are established, we post them throughout the entire house. Even in the bathrooms, the goals are there. We established that every morning. We still wake up to this day and see our goals. If we don't accomplish a certain goal, we leave it on the list for next year. We also keep track of our progress from year to year. We celebrate our accomplishments and push for better in the next year. Goal-setting keeps us inspired and focused. The results have been remarkable because they have transformed us into a family intentional about succeeding in every area of our lives. Setting goals helps a person maintain a level of integrity and accountability. My family has evolved and transformed over the years just because we intentionally plan to win year after year. I challenge you to do the same with your family. No matter how crazy it may seem you must plan to win. My brother-in-law used to be very shocked by the goals we had posted in the bathroom when he would come to visit. He thought it was a bunch of trash, but as he paid closer attention, he became inspired. He even encouraged other people to do the same thing because it had successfully worked for him. Goal-setting is a concept I talk about every chance I have when in the presence of people. Goal-setting is the cornerstone of sustained success.

I am grateful for my extraordinary family because we intentionally choose to be happy. We not only post our goals around the house but we also post positive pictures showing winning moments. Keeping these small victories in the forefront helps us keep the right attitude no matter what life brings our way. Now, don't get me wrong. We don't have a bunch of clutter around the house, but we do have clarity about where we are headed. We also can reflect on how God has truly blessed us and cherish those memories. When we look at those pictures, we can remember the happiness we felt in the moment. Having a loving relationship with your family where we honor, cherish and love one another is the heartbeat of our family. When fear or doubt tries to creep into our lives, we take a moment to reflect on our wins, celebrate the learning opportunities and look forward to our winning future.

We were not put on this earth to just pay bills, sleep, have fun, go to school and die. We were put here to fulfill a purpose. You have not truly collided with destiny if you aren't helping others. We were put here to transform other people's lives. One of the things near and dear to my heart is when I purchase a suit I always give one away. I don't think its right to hoard material things and not share them with loved ones or someone less fortunate. What's the use of having a gluttony of stuff hanging around knowing that I'm not using those things? I remember one amazing year when I first met my wife. I had her take all of her shoes and gave them away. She was shocked that I did that. I told her, "You know you weren't wearing them. There are a lot of people out there who need shoes. You will be blessed with an abundance of shoes in the future!" Right after that, she began receiving just as many shoes that we had given away. At the time she had about 300 pairs of shoes in her inventory worth over

$100,000. The shoes given away may cost anywhere from $200-$700 and now she walks around in shoes ranging from $1200-$10,000. My wife always says, "Won't He Do It!" And yes. God will allow you to experience true happiness when you make blessing others a priority. It's not the material things that make you happy but it's the blessing of being a blessing to others.

Going to the next dimension in life requires you to become a craftsman of your own life.

9

Beat on Your Craft

HAVE YOU EVER heard of the term, "hone your craft"? To hone is simply to sharpen or perfect a skill. I teach those in my sphere of influence to "beat on your craft." Some of you may be wondering, "What's my craft?" Your craft is any gift or talent that you possess that brings you financial gain and opens doors of opportunity for you. It's not enough to just go to school and obtain a degree, but if you don't continue to feed your brain with useful information for personal development, you will lose everything you have ever learned. Going to the next dimension in life requires you to become a craftsman of your own life. No one is responsible for making your life better. Only YOU have the power to perfect and develop your skills. Yes, you do need mentors and peers to help shine a light on any blind spots you may have, but it is totally up to you to reshape the "steel" in your life. Your character is who you are when no one is looking so you must perfect your character with each interaction with the human race and even when you are alone. Your integrity must be "beat" to perfection for you to truly maximize the doors of opportunities that are only available to you once certain areas of your craft has been perfected.

No one will make you beat on your craft, not even God. Whether you are a Reading Teacher or a Rock Star, store manager or Vice-President you must beat on your craft daily. Whether you are single or married, child or adult, young or old, you must carry yourself as if you are already on the level you are going to next.

I give you permission to embrace your differences. I give you permission to break down the barriers that keep you from growing, expanding, and learning how to grow and perfect the seeds God has put inside of you. God has given his permission to open ourselves up to relate to other like-minded people who also pride themselves on beating on their crafts. Evolution takes time, but with the right perspective, the right tools and the right community of influencers, you will be an UNSTOPPABLE force!

Many of you are frustrated and emotional as it relates to going to the next level in your craft, my friend, you do not have to overreact, be impatient or be reactionary because the situation always works itself out AFTER you have done everything you can do to make things better. Do not let your emotions be the catalyst for negative actions, reactions, and words. Negative actions are not only being belligerent, irate and ignorant but doing NOTHING as it relates to your craft, is just as detrimental as sending negative vibes into the universe. Allowing your gifts to lie dormant is just as harmful to your growth and personal development as being negative. You have to be the chief craftsman as it relates to your craft becoming perfected. No one is asking for you to be perfect, but the universe demands you to be intentional about beating on your craft and being your best even in your private life. Beat on your craft among your family and friends. PRACTICE, PRACTICE, PRACTICE. How do marching bands look so great during halftime? How do football teams prepare for Sunday games? How do supermodels walk so well on the runway during a show? PRACTICE, PRACTICE, PRACTICE! Read everything you can about your craft and watch every video imaginable. There was a time when information regarding certain skills could only be obtained in a college setting or if you were born into a certain family, but the information superhighway has made honing your craft as easy as a click of a button. You have NO

EXCUSE not to DOMINATE in the industry you have been called to serve.

Another critical component of beating on your craft is having the right people around you. How good can you be with the right people around you? You are only as successful as the five people closest to you. You will never know how good you can be no matter what I have said to you if you allow another year to go by without beating on your craft.

You have a major gift inside of you that needs to BLOSSOM to fulfill your purpose. The seeds inside of you are blooming right now. The incomparable M J said it best:

> *Just beat it, beat it, beat it, beat it*
> *No one wants to be defeated*
> *Showin' how funky and strong is your fight*
> *It doesn't matter who's wrong or right*
> *Just beat it, beat it*
> *Beat it, beat it, beat it*

© Written and Performed By: **Michael Jackson**

Your future is bright, and your craft is waiting for you to JUST BEAT ON YOUR CRAFT!

The testimonies that I am sharing are NOT for me to "toot my own horn" but to show you in real time how every encounter counts.

10

God Used Me as a Vessel

AS WE GO through life, it is important that we allow God to use us as vessels to be a blessing to others. Being a financial blessing to those in need is always admirable, but there are times when people need hope to simply get out of bed each day. Some people wake up depressed and go to bed the same way, and it is our duty to help another person collide with their purpose especially after we've become clear about ours.

I have had the opportunity to interact some with amazing people throughout my life. Many people have helped me along the way, but it's not about me. I realize it is my responsibility to help another person win at this game called, "Life" without apology or excuse!

This chapter shows proof of how God used the idea of "air" to flow through me to help people to fulfill their purpose in life. You will notice my name a lot throughout this chapter but this is not my way of being narcissistic or in need of accolades. Rather look at this as a template of what you want people to say about you before and after you leave this earth. I truly thank each and every one of them for providing and sharing some of their lives with me and now you. Why are there so many? Because I want you to pick the situation or story that you can best relate to. I wanted to frame this chapter to give a well-rounded understanding of how God uses you as a vessel to help people. When you read my name, please know that it's not me but God working through me. Because there's no way I could have done these things on my own. I trust that you will find a story that you can relate to in order to be inspired to help someone else.

You Believed In Me...

"...Thank you for all that you have done for me. You have no idea what you have done so let me explain. You gave me the opportunity to believe in myself, and that's one of the biggest things a human can do for another. My upbringing was filled with happiness, sadness, hurt, and a plethora of other feelings that one may have for the way they were brought up. Throughout that time, no one protected me nor consoled me, so I've learned to deal with those circumstances on my own when I was too young to even understand what was happening to me. I was a "stand out student" only because of my athletic abilities. I was always told not to talk about the things I've been through so that may explain why I act the way I do.

The very first day you walked into the store, I had no idea who you were or what major player you would become in my life. I'm forever grateful for that day. You got me out of so much. I've always been a "troublemaker" surrounded by drugs and anything else you can possibly think of. I always knew I deserved more than I was presented with at that time and that I could do better. But the only thing was, I didn't have anyone to help me realize the potential that I had in me.

You gave me the opportunity to come to Houston and work by simply believing that I had what it takes to succeed... Chaseray, you believed in me when I didn't believe in myself and were there when I felt alone. I had a miscarriage and kept it to myself because of how I was brought up. The only reason I mentioned it to you was because of my previous management team thinking otherwise. I told you that while holding back tears and you were so compassionate and understanding. I've never had that from anyone...ever!

Chaseray, from the bottom of my heart I just want to say thank you for everything you have done for me. I've never had anyone believe in me more than I believed in myself and you will never know how that makes me feel. You know my relationship with my dad, so you know that is non-existent. Thank you, Chaseray, for giving me all of the opportunities that you have provided for me. Thank you for believing in me. Thank you for just simply being you. You are truly God's child."

Can God trust you to be a vessel for Him to use to empower other people to live their best lives? We must look outside of ourselves and be compassionate towards one another. God using us as vessels to help each other is what being a part of the human race is all about!

Contagious Positivity...

"As a middle manager for a major clothing company, the direction from upper management has always been very reactive in nature. We have always been known as the problem solvers when things get bad. This led to a very negative mindset since we were always dealing with problems and only called in when the worst case scenario played out.

Our company went through an acquisition like many, and I would find myself reporting to yet another supervisor. Expecting the same routine when I received a call from Chaseray, I was blindsided! I knew immediately that this person would either break me or make me stronger. His demeanor was like no other that I had encountered in a supervisory role. He was always upbeat and motivating, accepting no excuses and coaching through every conversation. His positive demeanor was contagious, and I couldn't help but emulate his behavior, or at least my version of it so that I could hopefully make others feel just as encouraged as I did when interacting with him. This new mindset of positivity didn't just occur during the conversation; we would receive inspirational messages, videos, quotes and such when we least expected it, and they seemed to always come at the right time when we were feeling overwhelmed or frustrated. His timing was impeccable. And of course, this new mindset of mine couldn't help but spill over into my family life. My thoughts became increasingly positive, and my family noticed. My relationship with my husband and children was strengthened as a result, and more importantly, my relationship with God developed further as well. I see Chaseray treat every day and every conversation as if it is a gift and I too want to embrace life and get the most out of it as well. I truly believe that the power of positivity has transformed my marriage, my relationship with my children, my ability to manage more effectively and my growing relationship with God."

Can people speak well of how you've helped them improve? Positivity is contagious and you must be the catalyst to change any negative environments that you find yourself in. How do people perceive you? Do you cause them to retreat because of negative energy you may be displaying or do you saturate the universe with contagious positivity? The world is full of possibilities but we must first be ferociously positive no matter what! Below you will read the same person sharing the second part of their powerful testimony:

Change Is Inevitable...

"I just wanted to tell you that I got myself together after we last spoke. I was so surprised today at my own visceral reaction to hearing the news that you would no longer be my direct coach. I thought a lot about why I was so broken up over the news, and how shocking my reaction was to it. I'm not a person who cries. It takes a lot to get me to the point I was today. It didn't feel very professional and I was embarrassed that I seemed unable to control my own reaction...You also stated there were more missing from the book but do we really want to bore the reader with all of the people singing your praises? You had more influence over me than probably anyone in the last 10 years of my life and I suppose I had a reaction of fear. Fear and sadness and disappointment. But I finally realized something that you knew all along. Change is inevitable. I wish we had more time. But change is good. And inevitable. Period. I had no idea the impact you would have on my life...I suppose my fear is that I will go the rest of my career without ever having the chance to have a mentor/coach like you. Someone who cares about my development

not just my results. You are one of the absolute greatest people I have ever met in my life and I'm quite sure I will never meet anyone like you ever again. To truly be successful, I need to be open to the universe, and changes, and adapt to what comes my way. Clearly, the last time I thought I knew how things would go from this perspective, I was more wrong than I have ever been about anyone or anything in my life. I'm going to approach this [change] with an open heart and an open mind. Having you for the 24 months I have had you as my coach has done more for me as a person, as a leader, as a developer of talent, than any other experience in my life. I hope you know that you are one of **those** *people. One of those people that is a once in a lifetime kind of person. A once in a lifetime experience. I feel so lucky that we have had the time we have had together. I know that even though our time was shorter than I had wished, that I would probably stay for a very long time under you, that's simply not the way things are…and this will be yet another opportunity to grow, to change, to adapt. And if I have learned anything from you, it is that true growth comes from adapting to change, from learning what we can and applying those lessons in the future. And I want to thank you with every atom in my body. Thank you. For all you have taught me and will continue to teach me. For being my support system, for listening to me, for showing me how to be truly successful* **you need to care more about others**. *For showing me what it looks like to be successful, and loving, and kind, and intelligent, and patient. For teaching me not to get ahead of the universe. For all of the lessons that I will use for the rest of my life, not just professionally. Thank you. For everything.*

We must confront the fear of change. Change is going to happen, but there is nothing to fear when it is time to go to the next level. Embrace your next level! Look around you to see how you can help someone win on the level you are on and as you are promoted in your life, don't forget where you came from. You can be loving, kind, intelligent, patient AND successful. Making people a priority is not a suggestion; it's a necessity.

Here's a quick note from a young man looking for a fresh start:

"...you really saved my life by broadening my horizons and getting me out of that small town mentality...when I asked... you delivered, and I will always be thankful for your blessings. Maryland is where my new life [began] and it all started with a phone call. Your network was faster than the internet. Even though we haven't seen each other in a few years, it's all love and all good! Thanks for being a man of your word!"

Being impeccable with your word is a core value that every human being on the planet should have. Along with that, who you surround yourself with is just as critical. "Your network is faster than the internet" is one of the most extraordinary accolades I have ever encountered. It is imperative that our network is full of "lifesavers" whose priority is to show people how to move from a poverty mentality to abundance, love, faith and fearless living.

You never know if your first encounter with a person is the last encounter they will have on this earth. You never know if just your presence will lighten their load and lift their spirits. One day I had the opportunity to connect with a young entrepreneur, a barber who had hit a rough patch in his life. For me it was just another day at the HD Barbershop with Andre, however, allow me to share his thoughts about our encounter: *"I was working at a barbershop cutting hair, and another barber referred a new client [to me]. I knew the moment I started cutting this very well-dressed gentleman's hair; he was God's Angel. I didn't know how much of an Angel he was until I hit a rough spot in my life a few years later. That's when my new client gave me spiritual advice to help me overcome the things I was going through at that moment. I've learned a lot from my new client throughout the years of cutting his hair. He shared God's words with me. He gave me advice about [being] a better person and businessman. He gave me uplifting words on days when I knew it was God talking through him to get His message to me. I can go on & on talking about my client because he's very intelligent, smart, and very wise businessman. He's a Great and Awesome Father &*

Husband to his Beautiful Wife but more than anything he's God-fearing. He's more than a client to me. Now he's a man that I Respect...and I'm glad to know him as a person, and I'm very proud to be his barber...I'm talking about Chaseray Harvey."

To those who counted me out, THANK YOU FOR CALLING ME STUPID! I would not have been able to make a difference in this world just by walking in a room had I not been humiliated as a youngster. This "Teflon mentality" helps me and has the capacity to help you make a profound difference in this world no matter what you are going through. I can't say what was going through my mind when I encountered this young man, but I am confident of this: it is perfectly fine to be well-dressed on the outside but what you put in the atmosphere for others to consume is what will matter in the end. I cannot remember all of the advice that I've shared with him, but one thing is for sure when a person is better just because you walk into a room, that's how you know God is using you as a vessel even before you open your mouth.

The testimonies that I am sharing are NOT for me to "toot my own horn" but to show you in real time how every encounter counts. No encounter is an accident. You never know why you enter someone's life, but God knows. You are His hands and feet on earth. You were put here to show someone how to walk by faith and not by sight. Consider the words of these statements of gratitude from those assigned to my sphere of influence by God, Himself. Be inspired.

That Awkward Moment...

"It was awkward for a moment. I met my new Servant Leader over 8 years ago, and he couldn't appear more different from my previous leader or myself. This guy who I grew to respect and love as a person was loud and flamboyant and always the center of attention. Myself, reserved and usually happy to just soak in the scene. It was overwhelming at times. He would walk into a restaurant and vocally announce our presence like we were royalty. We would walk into management gatherings in retail stores or restaurants as if we were there to hold the meetings. We were

world-renowned speakers or famous in our fields. At least that was how he announced us…mostly me…It was funny, uncomfortable and in the beginning, I hated it.

As time passed and I grew to understand his impact on others and his outlook on the world and my perception completely changed. He found a way to break down the barriers with EVERYONE. He found a way to relate to EVERYONE. He could read a person in seconds. He followed a path to leave a true legacy by getting rid of the negativity and reach people on a personal level. Then he used that to teach and grow them to be better people. He even got me to dance a few times.

He developed a code of ethics for our team. We call it the "30 Steps". Of course it related to our business, but in reality, it was a path to a better life, provided communication skills that would work outside the work environment and helped everyone involved to develop and grow. He often said, "Don't get ahead of the universe." What he meant was if we focus on the 30 steps and learn how to use them and coach others to do so, over time you do not need to overreact, be impatient or be reactionary the problem will work itself out. It was a way to lead and not let emotions be the catalyst to the actions.

When I think of the word "integrity," I see a picture of Chaseray Harvey. He isn't always that loud and flamboyant guy that originally caught me off guard. He is an introspective, deep thinker. He reaches out often at 4 am with some great **"Just Thinking"** thought or an idea to help reach our team, or a way to think differently or view something differently, or to inspire…It is always something fresh and new and always informative and inspirational. He is someone you can truly trust. Our multi-unit team has evolved and changed over the years, but I can honestly say the entire group truly appreciates his leadership.

I don't know where our futures will take us, but I know he will always hold an important position not only in my growth and development but also in my heart. Hell, even my wife who is kinda hard to win over truly respects and appreciates the impact he has had on our lives. His legacy is already intact through all the lives he has touched. Thanks, Coach."

Jail Time...

"I met Chaseray 23 years ago. He helped me get my job that I have had for 23 plus years. He helped guide me into a wonderful career I love. He just gave me some advice and helped build my confidence even more. I did not know this man at all but I knew a female I worked with said the company is hiring and the guy that does the hiring is Chaseray Harvey. I called to see where he would be that day and came to see him. He interviewed and said, "You're a little shy...just make sure you give good eye contact on your next interview and smile." That's exactly what I did. I got the job. I called him the next day to thank him. From that moment on he played a very important role in my life. He's a guy you just want to hear what he had to say or what perspective he was thinking. He was always protective of me. When I first started there were only two females that worked in our market. He said to me, "Whatever you do with this company do not get a reputation it can hurt you." I followed his advice which I knew but it helped. I remember when I had outstanding driving tickets and went to jail I was terrified I would lose my job. I thought I was going to be there a while and I had no money to get out. I was sitting there terrified scared, dressed in business attire with [hardened] criminals and later on that day someone came and said, "Ma'am, someone just bailed you out." I was sitting there in disbelief thinking, "Who would do this for me?" Who knew I was there? Well to my relief it was Chaseray, laughing and I was thinking, "Dam, do who know what I just went through and why was he so happy?!" Well, I laughed, too, saying, "Yes! Thank you, Jesus! I'm free!" I was so happy. I explained what happened. Jokingly, all he said was, "I want my money back!" Another Highlight was a time I had been with the company for a while and I was going through a very tough time in my life. To this day that was the toughest time ever. I couldn't cope...I was so depressed. Chaseray finally came to my store, took me outside and said, "What the hell is going on?" I burst out crying and he was shocked to see I was so consumed with so [many] personal issues. Again, to my surprised he consoled me and said, "It's going to be alright, you're a soldier." Just him telling me that instead

of brushing my personal issues aside and not wanting to deal with that which I thought that was going to happen, he did the opposite and embraced me. He doesn't know but that helped me tremendously. He has been such a positive role model in my life. I respect him and appreciate all that he has done. I have seen him grow and do things other people can't even come close to like being up all night sending positive emails to encourage the team. He never takes a lot of time for himself because he is so giving to others. He is definitely an example when it comes to walking the walk and talking the talk. I really do believe somehow this man has Super Powers that God has given him because he has put so much positive energy into the universe. "Well-balanced" is what I think of when I think of him. A great man giving the universe a taste of his Super Powers!!!!!"

God used me as a vessel to help this young lady transform her life by using her OWN superpowers of focus, confidence, and faith. Yes, I did have to provide "tough love" at times, but that is a part of the seed planting process. Growth does not always feel good, and at times it seems dark and lonely, but you have the same gift inside of you to take charge of every learning opportunity presented to you. Never lose sight of the gifts that you have inside of you because the world needs you to WIN!

3 Things...

"Thank you! I want to think back seven years when I decided to end my career with my company. I will never forget what you said to me. And I quote..." You're just going on Sabbatical Leave." Chaseray, you believed and saw something in me even when I had doubts. That is why I am where I am today with my career, store manager...Your coaching has given me the ability to become a great leader. It is these 3 things that I got from you that has helped me along the way.

1. *Lead by example*
2. *Communicate effectively*
3. *Never stop improving*

Your leadership made it easy for me to become a better leader. Mr. Harvey, working for you is an honor. Working under your leadership is a pleasure, an experience that I will truly treasure."

No matter what industry you are a part of, you must lead by example. People are watching you whether you realize it or not. They study your strengths and weaknesses but the truth is how you effectively communicate is what helps them *apply* what you've taught them. People hear what you say and watch what you do. That is why you can NEVER STOP IMPROVING. Never give up on yourself no matter how tough things may seem.

Keep Fighting...

"I met Chaseray when I had just graduated high school I was working retail at the mall. Chaseray was my new manager. He was dressed in a burgundy 100 % polyester suit and carrying a black briefcase. I remember going home that day and telling my mom that I think his name is, "Chaseray." What a cool name! It didn't take long, but we became good friends. Chaseray was someone I looked up to and someone I wanted to be like. He was mentally strong. He had incredible drive and was going to be successful in everything that he did and to make others around him successful. He never gave up. He was a true competitor and always found ways to improve himself and those around him. [He had] incredible positive thinking and only expects the best...I have had lots of great memories shared with Chaseray. One that stands out was when I was trying to join the military. There were entry tests that needed to be taken. I didn't do that well, I was pretty upset, but Chaseray gave me some great words of wisdom, "It wasn't meant to be. God has other plans for you..." It's that kind of thinking that has shaped my life. Every time life brings challenges, and when I think I can't do it, I think about Chaseray and how you have to keep fighting and do the right thing and make most of every day. Thank you, Chaseray for being my friend and my Mentor."

Keep fighting no matter what life brings your way. Stay positive and know that everything that happens to you is for a reason. God has great plans for you, and I am excited to see what He does in your life!

A Lifetime Impact...

"An influential and positive person in my life...I consider him to be a great mentor and even better all-around person. It's not many people you cross paths with that have a lifetime positive impact on you, but I definitely cherish being able to have a relationship with someone as impactful as Chaseray. He entered my life at a pivotal time when I was 20 years old. I had just dropped out of college and had a son. I didn't know what my next move would be. I was working at a sports store at the time and just wasn't in a position to provide for my son like I wanted to. I reached out to Chaseray for an opportunity to work at his company. Chaseray not only gave me the opportunity but he mentored me and gave me great advice to be able to succeed in Management positions. He has always given me some type of great advice whenever we've had a conversation. He not only provides that great advice but he definitely lives it. He's a man of his word and wants the best for anyone he can help. He's definitely made a lifetime impact on me, and I challenge myself every day to be the same type of individual in others' lives just as he is in mine."

In today's world, there are so many experts that sell their advice to others who are on the fast track to success. What some fail to realize is you have to LIVE the advice you give. It's not enough to walk the earth critiquing other people when you aren't impeccable with your own word. Making a lifetime impact on another person's life can be done in a positive way as well as negatively. Never let it be said that you passed up the opportunity to help another person find their niche in life. There is nothing greater than finding the sweet spot of purpose. God has sent amazing people to show me the way, and now I challenge you to help others find their sweet spot in life. Who are you committed to helping this week? Take a moment and think about how you can go out of your way to help another person gain clarity about their purpose.

Synchronicity...

"Almost 20 years ago I met, who I called back then, the "Pied Piper" of retail. I was working for another retail store when I met him. We were getting a new store in our city, and he and his partner were out scouting for recruits for this new store. I didn't know it at the time; I just thought he was someone from our corporate office.

He told me that he was shopping for some "house slippers" for his little girl. I tried to assist, and he then told me who he was. He set me up with an interview the next day. I went to the interview, and 20 years later, I not only call him my boss but also my friend.

Chaseray is an amazing man. As he so often says, "I'm just looking for ordinary people who I can help do extraordinary things." I can truly say that he has done that for me. When I started working with him, I was shy and very timid around customers/people. Since that time I have overcome a lot of my shyness and timidity and accomplished a lot of things that I can thank him for pushing me and never giving up on me.

I won't say that we haven't had a few tough conversations and that we have always agreed on everything, but I can say this about him, he may not have the answer to everything, and he may not always have the right answer or solution, but he does something. He's going to try 'something.' He's not a quitter, and he NEVER gives up! He never settles for anything. If defeated he is already strategizing on how to get the 'next win.' He believes that a winner is in everyone, who wants to win. He makes you believe the impossible is possible if you believe. He teaches you to always sharpen your saw and utilize what you have in your 'toolbox' to your advantage.

He'll give you the script to help you be successful on the job and the motivation to take those same behaviors and skills and apply them to your everyday life. He has always been available, even as he has climbed the corporate ladder and has taken on more responsibility. Even through the tough and challenging times he has remained optimistic and had 'never let me see him sweat.' For those who are hungry, he will teach his team to fish, so that they will never go hungry.

He is charismatic, brilliant, funny, a family man who loves his wife and children. He has proven to be a great man whom I admire and respect.

The first meeting that I attended he talked about synchronicity. I believe that it was synchronicity that our paths crossed. Not only has this 'chanced meeting' help me gain some lifelong lessons, but it has also helped me gain a lifelong friend."

What a "WOW" moment! This testimony reminds us that "if you teach a hungry person how to fish, they will never go hungry." This wisdom transcends beyond the corporate world but even in your family, as you parent your children, teach them how to lead by being the lead servant among their peers. Quitting is NEVER an option when you are pursuing your purpose, and that's why I never give up on people. Even when it seems like they have given up on themselves, someone has to believe in them just like someone believed in me. Synchronicity is defined as, "the simultaneous occurrence of events that appear significantly related but have no discernible causal connection." In other words, everything that happens, happens at the right time, the right place and with the right people. Notice the theme among the testimonies? Our paths were synchronized before time began. Only an extraordinary God could do something so absolutely PHENOMENAL, and I am humbled at how perfect His timing is.

The Depth of Excellence...

*"I am reminded of a recent encounter in which Chaseray paid us a surprise visit to my store. He carried himself with such a **depth of excellence** until it instantly made me feel nervous and eager to make a great impression. He was so well fashioned! I instantly started to feel underdressed in my slacks and comfortable shoes. He exuberates confidence but yet he stepped right in to assist the store and was eager to leave staff, such as myself, encouraged. Though he carries himself with such responsibility and class, he is still a down to earth kind of guy that commands respect with his presentation. This particular day my purpose was sort of on the backburner. Mr. Chaseray's words were as I quote, "God sent me here for you today."*

*That one encounter with Mr. Chaseray shifted me into **instant*** *motivation to pursue purpose. I have been liberated by the inner light that shines through Mr. Chaseray from the inspirational emails he sends, the sense of humor he carries along with him, and the great balance of patience, stewardship, and sternness to keep our company's standards.*

I have always seen a man of integrity in Mr. Chaseray, however, after talking personally with him at our Woodlands store recently, I saw that he's a man who respects and honors God for all of his success and abilities. He is also a man with a heart to help others."

The term "depth of excellence" carries tremendous weight with me because I try to carry myself with dignity everywhere I go and in everything I do. The words I put out into the universe can only be positive because that is what I expect everyone around me to experience. Excellence, positivity and the motivation to pursue purpose in a greater measure.

We All Have Different Gifts

*We all have different gifts that God has given us. Chaseray Harvey has the gift of encouragement. Time and time again, Chaseray has been a positive supporter and cheerleader in my career. He has the ability to see the gifts and talents within an individual thus allowing them the freedom to be their best. Through his **endless demonstration of belief** in you, his positive and encouraging words, he has contributed to the success of others by allowing them [to have] a platform to excel. This passage of scripture comes to mind when thinking of Chaseray Harvey and his leadership; **Romans 12: 2- 8 states;***

Do not conform any longer to the pattern of this world, but be transformed by the renewing of your mind. Then you will be able to test and approve what God's will is- his good, pleasing and perfect will. For by the grace given me I say to every one of you: Do not think of yourself more highly than you ought, but rather think of yourself with sober judgment, in accordance with the measure of faith God has given to each of you. Just as each of us has one body with many members, and these members do not all have the same function so in Christ we who are many form one body. And each member belongs

to all the others. We have different gifts, according to the grace given us. If a man's gift is prophesying , let him use it in proportion to his faith, If it is serving , let him serve, if it is teaching , let him teach; if it is encouraging, let him encourage; if it is contributing to the needs of others, let him give generously; if it is leadership, let him give diligently.

The above-mentioned passages illustrate that God's will for each of us is good and perfect. God commands us to not think too highly of ourselves and be humble. The ability to understand and recognize the gifts of others is paramount to being a strong leader. It is even more important to recognize those gifts that differ in any form or manner than your own and that they are still valuable gifts. We all have different gifts, and we are all diversified in our own way in which God created us. The journey of life we are on is a mix with many peaks, valleys and a lot in between. I perceive it as an open book, large with many blank pages just sitting above us waiting for the next chapter, paragraph, and sentence to be written. It will be written from beginning to end. There is no way around it. What will it read? Will it be said; "that I gave my best"? I believe that through Christ I will achieve all things. Where will your journey lead you? Someone over time has said, "Much is demanded from those who have much to offer." Inside each of you is something SPECIAL. Gifts that were given to you: and for you alone. Embrace the gifts that are yours. Use these gifts to achieve what you were meant to achieve. To achieve something special it will take something and someone special. That someone is you. In some cases, in order to achieve something special, someonehad to believe in you and honestly expect nothing more from you than you and your gifts. That is rare. Chaseray possesses this trait. In one conversation, Chaseray and I had, he asked me what I attribute my success to. I answered with confidence what I BELIEVE it to be. In that moment he did not flinch but smiled and agreed. He recognized the gifts that I had and embraced them. That is my Chaseray Harvey story. Favor from above and someone here [on earth] believing in me and encouraging me along the way."

Another powerful "WOW" moment. We are all responsible for posturing ourselves with an endless demonstration of a positive belief system. We must not allow negativity to penetrate our perspectives, goals or legacy. The Good Book says, "To whom much is given, much is required." It's imperative that we stop taking our responsibility to inspire one another as a suggestion only. We are to be relentlessly kind to one another and bring out the best in each other. We all have gifts that were planted in us. Not only are our gifts unique to our DNA but our gifts are for the advancement and enhancement of those in our sphere of influence.

"As I reflect on my tenure working with you, my mind is flooded with memories that came with joy, laughter, pain, and growth. Your leadership, coaching, correction, mentorship, trust, encouragement, loyalty and your words of wisdom have propelled me into the business savvy woman I am today.

Starting at an entry-level position of a Customer Service Associate into Management, I learned to trust your guidance for my career. You spoke some of the most profound words [to me] such as, **"This is a good move for you", "You can make your mark here", "It's going to take you about five years to grow into your position", "Don't put your feelings into an email, get to the point", "This move is going to take your career to another level", "Your career is going to soar when you make this move".** *All of the words you've spoken proved to be true.*

When I faced obstacles, and later, tragedy hit my family, you encouraged me and coached me through, never giving up on me and recognizing my potential early on. You said, **"Nothing is built overnight."** *As you reflected back to when the company was first started in the back of a pickup truck, I could write a book about you myself. I'm forever grateful that God allowed our paths to connect. You are a true and living example of a servant leader."*

Take a moment to reflect on a Servant Leader who has left a memorable mark on your life. If possible, reach out to them and thank them for the lessons you've learned, the doors of opportunity they have opened to you and/or the mentorship they have provided.

Human beings are God's greatest resource in the world. The easiest way to preserve the human race is by spreading gratitude like its CONTAGIOUS!

I wish I could truly articulate how truly blessed I am to live on this earth at this moment in time. It is no accident that you are reading this. YOU MATTER to this world, and if you haven't started working on the things you know you have been called to do, it's time to go to work... NO EXCUSES! God planted a seed in you that should never go to waste. A winner lives inside of everyone who wants to win, so I ask you, do you want to win or do you want to make excuses? Listen closely; this chapter is NOT about me; it is all about YOU living the most extraordinary life you could possibly live. I trust that these positive words are helping to fuel your fire to freedom in your God-given purpose. God is looking for extraordinary people to do extraordinary things.

My challenge to you is to discover how you can be used as a vessel for the enhancement and empowerment of the people in your sphere of influence. In what ways are you going to unify and influence individuals to become better people who will impact nations? In what way will you provide faith infusions when it seems there is no hope? Don't feel bad if you are still trying to figure out how to make your mark on society. God can and will use you if you are willing to accomplish extraordinary things in your own life. I shared these heartfelt testimonies with you to show you that even though there are some people who may call you stupid or mistreat you or simply refuse to celebrate you, there are some people who will actually cherish you.

Keep your heart pure, your hands clean and be grateful. God wants to use you as a vessel if you are willing to say, "Yes" to transforming lives for as long as you live. I am humbled at how God has used me as a vessel to help transform lives, and if you haven't started yet, now it's your turn.

Rise, shine and show the world your greatness!

The Conclusion: Thank You for Calling Me Stupid

I did not write this book to expose anyone nor to be rude; however, I want you to know that my transparency could be the key to your next dimension. If I can be honest and transparent about my past decisions, it may help someone else do the same. There is something freeing about being transparent. Becoming transparent is a key ingredient if you want to make an indelible mark on history. I needed to share with you where I have been so that you could visualize the journey with me of where you and I are headed. I am on a continued quest to change peoples' lives in magical ways. So many people live their lives out of routine or tradition, but life is given for us to live it to the fullest! We must be fully present and be in alignment with what we were put here on earth to do. Do not leave this world without making a positive impact on history. Your footprint and timestamp should leave a blueprint for your children's children to know you were here leaving an undeniable legacy of love, discipline, harmony, peace, and prosperity. Many people put great emphasis on their educational credentials and the extent of their knowledge, but just like a tape measure, credentials and knowledge can only extend so far. Many of us have a wide range of life experience, but even that can only go so far if we refuse to pay it forward. It's not enough to have a wealth of life experience, but we must share knowledge and wisdom to inspire people to become better. We must activate the invisible possibilities inside of every human we encounter. You have the power to make a positive impact and change peoples' lives for the better.

Another reason I wrote this book was to encourage you to learn to value true friendship. An example of true friendship is when a person shares a life-changing book like this one or audio recording for personal development for you to gain a deeper understanding of yourself, society and the world at large. My experiences as a child, adolescent, teen and young adult are filled with a variety of struggles and challenges that could have left me bitter. For example, when I was arrested due to racial profiling, even though it was unfair I decided not to let moments like that define who I was. I could have continued to make it a race issue, but as I evolved as a successful businessman who interacts with people of all races, I choose not to see things in a negative light. I see things that have occurred in my life as putting me on a path to greatness. I could've continued to wallow in the things I have done wrong as well as the things I was wrongfully accused of, but at the end of the day, those situations didn't break me. Everything that happened to me and you were not put in our lives to break us but to transform us into the people we are becoming. I would not change anything about my past, not even the things I regret because without those life experiences, I would not have the level of understanding about life that I have now. I could have allowed my past to destroy me, but instead, I used the wisdom I've gained to elevate me in order to help others. I have the privilege of making a positive impact on the world around me and so can you. We must come together to transform the entire world in order to make it a better place. There is nothing "stupid" about the notion of harmony and world peace. In fact, this should be the goal every human should have. I pray this book has made you think about how you can use your past to help shape another person's future. I am so excited about my future, and I challenge you to become excited about yours. I am looking forward to a zillion years into the future with my amazing wife of over two decades. I am looking forward to loving her in this life and even in the afterlife. Who are you going to spend the rest of your life with helping to change the world? You don't have to be in a romantic relationship to impact the world, but it is imperative that you embrace true friendship in order to make a magical impact on others for a positive future. We were born to accomplish purpose each and every day. You may have a similar journey as I've had or yours may be completely different, but one thing is for sure, we have all struggled in our own way. Here's the good news, you have the opportunity to redefine your life without judgment, routine or tradition. Many of us are stuck in our old ways of thinking, being and doing but those boring routines and traditional habits you may be engaged in must be abolished. It's time for us to create new traditions and break the routine so we can embark on an evolution that will change the world.

I challenge you to purchase this book for someone else now that you've read it. I pray this book helped you transform and discover the seed inside of you just like it did for me while writing it. Believe it or not, everything we desire is inside of us. God systematically made us a resource to produce our own heart's desires. So many individuals like doctors, lawyers, engineers, teachers, athletes, mothers, fathers all possess this ability. The ingredients are inside of us to be successful, and all we have to do is put the work in and transform into whatever we want to be. You hear people say, "Always believe in yourself!" And what happened to them? They transformed into great people. And don't believe the people who say you can't do something. Human beings have unlimited possibilities. Why? We can transform anything over time. Advancements in society prove it every day. Look at the skyscrapers, roads, lights, rockets, cell phones, computers, MRI machines, cars and the like. There are so many resources that are inside of you right now.

Look at it from this perspective; a single apple seed, that small brown seed. God systematically packed inside of it an entire tree! WOW! Yes, a tree! That single seed has over 500+ apples inside it. Are you kidding me? No! Believe it or not, God made us the same way, but 97% of the population don't realize that we are just like that apple seed. All you have to do is plant the seed in good soil and nourish it. It will be transformed into a tree over time and eventually an apple tree orchard. Now, that you know how to plant, nurture, and cultivate the seed inside of you, it will go through a metamorphosis and bloom into something extraordinary. Thank you for calling me stupid because you didn't know God planted the seed inside me and now it is in full bloom. Now, that we know this, look out because my best days are in front of me!

My wife, Mattie, expanded my mind by how she helped transform me into something even more than I thought was possible. She stated to me, "Your boundaries are created by your mind, and if you believe in yourself and you believe in your purpose of what you are going to do, anything can be accomplished." We are the ones who hold ourselves back from accomplishing our lifelong dreams. We must let go of the steering wheel of life and let God take the wheel and lead us in the way He desires for us to go. We don't accomplish our goals just by controlling our actions, but we must also activate the statement, "Walk by faith, not by sight" and the more that you declare that statement over your life, the faster your lifelong dreams will come to pass. Do good and slowly good will follow you. God has created us just like He created all things and we must read His manual (The Bible) to truly understand what He thinks about us and our future. It is vitally important that we understand that sometimes our parents, teachers, colleagues, and supervisors can be stumbling blocks when negative things are spoken over our lives. Sometimes they tell you that you can't accomplish something, but oftentimes they say that, not from a place of hate, but based on their own limitations. That may not be the case for everyone but for some people like myself that is a reality. Sooner or later over time, you began to believe the lies that you are stupid or you cannot accomplish your life goals. Some of you may have received a low grade from an English teacher or any teacher. Just remember that failure does not define you! Don't allow anyone to define you as a failure! Some of the same people who specialize in tearing you down are nowhere near achieving the great life you are destined to live. Don't believe anything that doesn't empower you! I was created by my Lord and Savior, and it is very clear that He's the only one who can define us. He made us in His image. I challenge you to read your Bible every day, and you will see you're being transformed into an exceptional person. So often we don't read the manual for electronics, our cars or our appliances then we complain about why the appliance is not operating properly. But the answer is very clear. It's because we never took the time out to read how the manufacturer created the device and understand how it really works. If we take the time to read the manual for our lives, we would see the value of what life really has to offer.

I thank everybody who called me stupid and underestimated me because, in actuality, you brought out the best in me. Stop what you are doing right now and make sure someone else is inspired by this book. Don't let anybody take advantage of you anymore. It's very clear that you are in total control and you have the success tools from this book to lead you to the life you truly desire to live. Don't let society determine what is placed on your mental hard drive that will misguide you in life. What you currently see on your hard drive is not the purpose inside of you. Many of you can tell right now you are not in purpose because the things you are feeling and doing right now don't satisfy you. I hope the stories I have shared impact you in a way that provokes change. No matter the odds that I have faced, I was able to overcome them and survive through all of them. I want to thank my siblings for preparing me to be successful in life in ways that they did not prepare themselves. They had no idea that every day they were shaping my life by giving me the armor I needed to persevere when life would attempt to crush me. I want to thank my mother, Evelyn, and father, Julius, for being two great examples of people working hard and with the highest degree of integrity. My parents are responsible for transforming my siblings and me, Curtis, Keith, Kennith and Julius and Sherry to men and women who love their family. My parents did the best they could to raise the incredible men and woman my siblings, and I have become. Regardless of their humble beginnings and educational background, they did the best they could do. I am so thankful that this book has come to fruition so that they have the opportunity to read and share in the accomplishments that I and my lovely wife, Mattie, and children have attained. I want to thank my entire family Cassandra, Tim, and Madison for your love and support over the years. I excited about passing the baton on to my children by leaving an amazing legacy of life lessons I have learned through the things I have experienced. I am grateful for everyone who has made major contributions not only to my life in general but to this book in particular. The amazing stories and life lessons I have learned are priceless, and I am so grateful that I had the opportunity to share them with you. I am grateful to God for always guiding me and for Jesus Christ who died on that old rugged cross for me. I trust that the highlights of my life story are not only a blessing to you but the learning opportunities outlined in this memoir will change the code and fabric of society. I trust that the seeds that have been implanted in each person reading this book begin to spring forth and come alive to reach the masses. I trust that men and women will be able to evolve in a greater measure for them to persevere in any situation that they will face in life. It is not the things that you've done right that taught you most; it is the things you did wrong and how people treated you that made us wise. *Thank You For Calling Me Stupid* continues in book #2. A lot has happened since I wrote this book. To those who called me stupid, THANK YOU! God not only planted a seed in me, but there is one inside of you, too.

About the Author

Chaseray Harvey is a dream coach and passionate author who serves as Servant Leader of one of the world's most renowned fashion brands and has been impacting lives in the industry since the 1980s. He currently resides in Houston, Texas with his wife Mattie where they are the Founders of P.E.P Texas with his wife Mattie where they are the Founders of P.E.P Houston, better known as, The **P**eople **E**nhancement **P**rogram. This extraordinary endeavor was created to empower, unify and rally individuals together by creating lifechanging charity balls and other events to help individuals and families experiencing financial hardship due to cancer and other lifethreatening illnesses.

Chaseray is the proud father of Cassandra and Madison. He enjoys playing sports, morning walks with his wife and dog, traveling along with sharing new experiences with family and creating new memories on a daily basis. Chaseray has an immense love for God and is convinced that without faith, nothing is possible.

Made in the USA
Coppell, TX
16 December 2019